THE OUTRAGEOUS PURSUIT OF HOPE

THE OUTRAGEOUS
PURSUIT OF HOPE

Prophetic Dreams for the Twenty-first Century

Mary C. Grey

DARTON · LONGMAN + TODD

First published in 2000 by
Darton, Longman and Todd Ltd
1 Spencer Court
140–142 Wandsworth High Street
London SW18 4JJ

ISBN 0–232–52319–3

A catalogue record for this book is available from the British Library

Designed by Sandie Boccacci
Phototypeset in 11¼/14pt Bembo
by Intype London Ltd
Printed and bound in Great Britain
by Page Bros, Norwich, Norfolk

This book is dedicated to all my friends and colleagues in Wells for India:

to Ramsahai, our great friend, who was the first to inspire us with Gandhi's vision of peace and sustainable living, and his family who welcome us all to their home; to the Tyagis in Jodhpur, who also keep the vision alive for us; to Peter, Veronica and their family and the memory of Dominic; to Robert, Sue, Rebecca and Pat; Jon and in memory of Gill; David and Frances, Alexina and Marcus, Hugh, Carol, Jonathan and Adam, Brian, Terry, Angela and Fiona, Helen, Gillian, Anne, David and Gillian, John, Isabel and Rosalind, Bob and Maureen, and all those who have journeyed with us into the desert of Rajasthan, and those who supported us at home. And most of all to Nicholas, life companion, *who keeps hope alive that the desert really will blossom and that its people will flourish . . .*

CONTENTS

LIST OF ILLUSTRATIONS

Illustrations between pp. 52–53

1. 'The children speak it; the last word. Hope.' The children of the Asha Project, Rajasthan, India. (Photograph: Mary Grey.)
2. 'A Dance in the Shadow of Death.' The power of ritual in a spirituality of resistance. (Photograph: © Mike Gold-water/Network.)
3. 'The Peaceable Kingdom' by Edward Hicks shows how the prophetic imagination of Isaiah has been inspirational in a vastly different historical context. (Philadelphia Museum of Art, Pennsylvania/Bridgeman Art Library, London.)
4. 'Once upon a time there was wisdom (*Sophia*), and she was present everywhere with all the intensity and all the desire of all there was. . . .' ('Sophia' by Robert Lentz.)
5. Jesus learnt from his mother Mary, Daughter of Wisdom (*Sedes Sapientiae*), as she had learnt from her mother, the St Anne of tradition. (Masaccio and Masolino, 'Madonna and child with St Anne', Galleria degli Uffizi, Florence/Bridgeman Art Library, London.)
6. The Trinity in the form of three rabbits in ceaseless, circular motion is an image suggesting that the entire creation reveals the beauty of God. (Stained glass window, Long Melford Church, Suffolk.)

INTRODUCTION

I wrote this book in the context of war. As I delivered, in Salisbury Cathedral, the inaugural Sarum Lecture Series on which the book is based, Nato was dropping nightly bombs in Serbia, and the refugee camps were already swollen with homeless families; their grief and stories of brutal killings were the painful background to this narrative. This context gave a grim seriousness to the question as to what could be the grounds for hope at the end of the second millennium. The fact that the First World War at the beginning of the century began with an assassination in Serbia, whereas it ends with the daily destruction of the country, highlights even more the prophecy that 'the lamps are going out over Europe: we shall not see them lit again in our lifetime'.[1]

I begin my reflection with two images. The first is a picture in the Tate Gallery:[2] it is a nineteenth-century painting by George Frederick Watts and shows a young girl, blindfolded, sitting on the globe, with a lyre. The caption is simply 'Hope' – and it features as the cover of this book. But anything less hopeful would be hard to imagine. Why such grief over the earth in a picture coming from a hundred years ago, when allusions to environmental disasters were not in the air, when time was not seen as running out? In fact, it was rather a time of optimism, arising from the acceptance of the theory of evolution, with the beginnings of the myth of endless progress and of the unstoppable development of western society.

The second image is its obverse. It recalls the Greek myth of Pandora,[3] who, it will be remembered, specifically against instructions, allowed all the evils of the world out of the box, until only one thing was left – namely, hope. Even if this is clearly another exemplar of the same ancient mythic pattern as the Hebrew Adamic myth, whose legacy still scapegoats women for evil in the world, yet Pandora's actions will yet be redeemed because earthly existence must always be grounded in hope. My first image, the blindfolded girl, symbolises a world having given up on hope: she cannot even utter the lament which the crisis calls for; like the Jews who hung up their harps on the willows of Babylon, she cannot play. I suggest that she throws into sharp relief the dilemma of these end-of-millennium times.

APOCALYPSE NOW!

The motif of apocalypse now hangs heavily in the air. For this is the way in which we are encouraged to understand our context by the media, the hype in Britain about the Millennium Dome,[4] films like *Armageddon*, hysteria about the Millennium bug about to destroy our computers and especially by the increasingly urgent warnings that time is running out for the planet. It is the aim of this book to explore a way through the labyrinth of doom and gloom, both the false prophecies and the unheeded warnings, the *fin-de-siècle* pessimisms, and the fears that time is running out for the universe.

The two threads weaving in and out of these lectures will be, first, that of *hope*, outrageous hope, hope beyond all reason, beyond emotion and even beyond all anger at injustice; a hope that is fully mindful of how this century began, with 'the lights going out over Europe', and now asks itself how to keep them flickering on, as we witness the lights going out again over Sarajevo, over Central America in the wake of Hurricane Mitch, and now, yet again, at the time of writing, over Kosovo – in fact, in the context of realisation that the culture of this dying millennium has reached its lowest ebb.

The second, and linked, thread is that of *prophecy*, a prophecy kneaded from critique, lament and vision, all these three being ingredients of a theology of hope. And our dialogue partner will be the Jewish prophet Isaiah. This is because Isaiah – or at least the book of Isaiah as we have it – lived in times of imminent disaster and the threat of the destruction of the city and Temple of Jerusalem; but then, after the destruction, when the worst had actually happened, and the children of Israel were forced to live in captivity in Babylon, it was the prophetic task to keep hope alive in the shadow of, the context of oppression, symbolised through the image of the Beast in the Book of Revelation.

Even after the exiles returned to Jerusalem, there had to be yet another way to rediscover hope. Because the Book of Isaiah is controversial in terms of which prophecies are authentically Isaiah, and which have been revised in the light of later events, it presents a field of tension between hope fulfilled, hopes shattered and hope deferred. Christianity has always been in love with Book of Isaiah – so much so that it has almost been regarded as a 'Fifth Gospel', as a recent book puts it.[5]

And, finally, I dialogue with the text of Isaiah, because it was in the context of the great 'Jubilee' agenda of Isaiah (to set the captives free and to preach the good news to the poor), that Jesus of Nazareth understood his mission and ministry, according to Luke 4:18f. I want to set up this dialogue deliberately in an inter-faith context (Isaiah has great meaning for the Jewish community), and in the context of the current Jubilee 2000 campaign to cancel Third World debt. So, hope, prophecy – and a third thread will be spirituality, because our theology is but straw, in the famous words of St Thomas

Aquinas, if it is not grounded in daily living. My question will be: what are the tools (disciplines or practices) of a spirituality for apocalyptic times? What are the tools that enable sparks of hope to keep burning despite hopelessness?

In Chapter 1 I focus on what it means to hope outrageously in the time of apocalypse, in times when it seems that that hope is offered only to those who can join in the culture of spending. In response, I explore what it means to live a spirituality of attending to time. Chapter 2, 'Crying freedom when the dream has died', asks how we are to keep alive a dream of justice and peace for humanity and all creatures, and explores a spirituality of resistance. The third chapter asks what the role of imagination is in this quest, linking the flourishing of human and earth communities with the inspiration of Isaiah's vision of the desert's blossoming. Chapter 4 considers the role of the Spirit on the brink of the third millennium – is there a new language to be discovered? The final chapter reflects on the figure of Wisdom, both inviting a female imaginary[6] of the divine, and evoking another kind of theological learning. The Isaian image of wisdom's feast is seen to be prophetic of a eucharistic ecclesiology. Through the figure of Wisdom, different dimensions of spirituality are interwoven and integrated, all as ingredients in *the outrageous pursuit of hope*.

'IN MY BEGINNING IS MY END': APOCALYPSE AND THE REBIRTH OF TIME

T. S. Eliot's words introduce the exploration of this chapter.[1] This time/space conjunction, the brink of a new millennium, creates a sense of mixed messages. There is an expectation, an openness, to new possibilities, as well as a sense of hopelessness and despair that nothing has been learned or gained in the course of the history of the second millennium. Above all, there is a sense that this is a unique moment: we are unwilling that its significance slip from our fingers.

But, what is the key which opens up an understanding of time for our culture? Should we look to the great cultural symbols of the age as a clue? It is difficult to avoid the conclusion that domes and Disneyland have become the great cultural symbols of the end of the century, and that supermarkets now spring up like glittering parodies of great medieval cathedrals. It seems sadly ironic that these new 'cathedrals' are even acquiring a spirituality. *Tesco ergo sum*, it is said. Shopping is our number one hobby, as frequent surveys point out. In the recent opening of the Bluewater Shopping Centre in Kent, it was even suggested that shopping should be a spiritual experience.[2]

But it is premature to give way to despair, to conclude that time has run out for the noblest expression of the human spirit. My invitation to the reader is not to join in what has been called by the American feminist theologian Sharon Welch 'the cultural despair of the middle classes',[3] but to see ourselves as in the time of *kairos*, times of intense significance, God's time, truly a time of apocalypse, seen not now as doom, but as revelation or the unveiling of God's purpose for us here and now. As John Paul II put it in his great encyclical *Tertio Millennio Adveniente*, announcing a Jubilee for the millennium, 'In Christianity time has fundamental importance.'[4] But before exploring what this offered *kairos* might mean, let us first consider the fundamental quality of hope that grounds not only human existence, but that of the survival of all earth's creatures.

HOPING BEYOND HOPE

African women, writes the Ghanaian woman theologian Mercy Amba Oduyoye, 'wear hope like a skin'.[5] The more desperate a situation is, the stronger the hope. We live by hope, says St Paul. Hope stretches the limits of what is possible. It is linked with that basic trust in life without which we could not get from one day to the next. It is, literally, the learned confidence that food and nurture will come, regularly, that encourages the new baby to thrive. Without this sense of possibility, writes William Lynch, 'we do not act or function. There is no energy.'[6] To live by hope is to believe that it *is* worth taking the next step: that our actions, our families, our cultures and societies have meaning, are worth living and dying for. Liturgically speaking, it is hope that gives us the energy, simply, 'to keep the feast', day in and out, year after year, to celebrate the seasons' dying and rebirth as part of God's creative plan. Conversely, to be without hope is to be trapped. It is to be helpless, to have no sense that it is worth getting out of bed, or taking a decision.

Living in hope says to us, 'There is a way out', even from the most dangerous and desperate situations, and we saw this with the amazingly courageous stories of the hostages Brian Keenan and John McCarthy.[7] But hopelessness means living from the sense of 'There is no way out', there is 'no exit', (the title of Jean-Paul Sartre's play, *Huis Clos*). This is frequently the case with people who are seriously mentally ill or suffering from a psychosis: the collapse of all possibilities, the merging into futility and sense of no future, is one scenario of the death of hope.

Another image captures this for me: the Chinese writer Han Suyin, (known for her biographies of Mao Tse Tung and for the novel *The Many-Splendoured Thing*), describes travelling, as a child, on a train through vast flooded valleys of China. For mile after mile she saw small stunted trees projecting from the floods. And to her horror she saw that there were people in these trees, thousands of people just waiting for death, people for whom hope and help would never come.[8]

What is it, then, that keeps hope alive in the most desperate of circumstances? Why did the woman in the recent tragedy in Honduras and Nicaragua cling on to a raft for six days and survive? Why did the playwright Susan Sontag decide to go to Sarajevo during the recent war in Bosnia and stage the play *Waiting for Godot*? Sarajevo, a city which, in the bitter struggles between Christian and Muslim, seems almost by itself to render meaningless the arrogance of modernism; and a play which seems to be the essence of the death of hope, as the two characters, the tramps Vladimir and Estragon, have to end each day stunned by the news of the messenger, 'Mr Godot isn't coming today'.

As the bombs fell on the city of Sarajevo, the actors had to risk snipers' bullets to get to the theatre; Sontag relates that their emaciation and lack of energy made great difficulties for rehearsing, as any time there was a break, they would lie down on the stage with exhaustion. Yet Dzevad Karahasan wrote about the experience:

> *Waiting for Godot* opened, with twelve candles on the stage ... There were two performances that day ... In Sarajevo there are only matinees; hardly anybody goes out after dark. Many people were turned away ... I think it was the end of the (third) performance ... during the tragic silence of the Vladimirs and the Estragons which follows the announcement 'Mr Godot isn't coming today, but surely will come tomorrow,' that my eyes began to sting with tears. Velibor was crying too. No-one in the audience made a sound. The only sounds were coming from outside the theatre, a UN AOC thundering down the street and the crack of sniper fire.[9]

It would be facile to make unwarranted generalisations on the basis of this one, tragic experience. Sarajevo, along with Auschwitz, the Menin Gate at Ypres, Saigon, Omagh in Northern Ireland, the Gaza Strip in Palestine, and now the ghost city of Pristina, capital of Kosovo, have become places of apocalyptic meaning for this century. Yet places of intense suffering can become places where the very nature of hope is revealed − its vulnerability, yet its power to gather up the fragments of shattered community, shattered humanity, and devastated nature. In the tragic coalescing of time and place, it is still possible, as Isaiah knew, for a people who walk in darkness to witness to a great light (Isaiah 9:2).

It was in the wake of the so-called 'death of God' movements, when it was felt that after Auschwitz no speech about God was possible, exactly then, after the Second World War, a theology of hope as such began to emerge. Slowly, falteringly, people began to speak of experiencing 'the beyond in our midst', of God as 'that which concerns us ultimately', as the great Thou addressing us from the heart of creation. It was in 1964 that Jürgen Moltmann's *Theology of Hope* appeared.[10] We owe a tremendous debt to this theologian, who dealt what I believe to be a death-blow to much of traditional theology, which saw the fulfilment of God's promises as only belonging to the end-times, and these end-times to be beyond history: 'Men [*sic*] became victims of a transcendental eschatology which once again obscured rather than developed the discovery of early Christian eschatology.'[11] Eschatology, study of the end-times, is for Moltmann a theology of hope, and hope must be grounded in history.

Building on this, from Latin America originally, but then from all parts of the world, came the great cry that our God is a God of the poor, vulnerable and oppressed, God is the great passion for justice who empowers and sustains all the movements for freedom and a transformed society. Liberation theology, although constrained and battered by events in certain parts of the world, has now become far more mature, responding to diverse contexts, taking on board and responding to the critiques of both feminist and ecological theologians.[12]

But this was only the beginning of the odyssey of hope. It is not difficult to keep faith with a God of justice when the freedom movements are successful. But it is when the revolution fails, despair sets in, and the dreams are shattered (today's revolutionaries becoming tomorrow's vigilantes, as the Philippino theologian Ed de la Torre has said[13]) – and, on a personal level, when people have to face a future of unemployment, poverty, and isolating caring for severely disabled dependants – that the discovery of a God who suffers with us, who becomes vulnerable with us, is what sustains our hope.[14]

Rediscovering the God of the covenant nurtures this hope, a God who assures us: 'Nor will I ever again destroy every living creature . . .'

As long as the earth endures,
  seedtime and harvest, cold and heat,
summer and winter, day and night,
  shall not cease.

(Genesis 8:21b–22)

But is not this precisely what is called into question in apocalyptic times – whether the world *will* endure or not? And this is why Isaiah is such a crucial dialogue partner. Simply look at the scale of the disaster which threatens the kingdom of Judah (remember the northern kingdom of Israel had already fallen):

The earth shall be utterly laid waste and utterly despoiled;
  for the Lord has spoken this word.
The earth dries up and withers,
  the world languishes and withers . . .
The earth lies polluted
  under its inhabitants;
for they have transgressed laws,
  violated the statutes,
  broken the everlasting covenant.
Therefore a curse devours the earth,
  and its inhabitants suffer for their guilt.

(Isaiah 24:3–6)

It is vital that we make the same connections that Isaiah does. When humanity ignores and tramples on the earth's own laws and rhythms – this is ecological sin, ecological injustice – then the very possibility of planetary survival is removed. Social life is destroyed. Isaiah goes on to say that the 'wine dries up', and all merriment, singing, conviviality is vanished. It is not just a question of agricultural, village life:

The city of chaos is broken down,
  every house is shut up so that no one can enter.

(Isaiah 24:10)

City life is ruined and all business deals are corrupted: for 'the treacherous deal very treacherously'. A grim picture prompting the cry of desperation: how can hope be sustained when the very possibility of life is removed? I suggest this is exactly the down-side of the cry of apocalypse, when, as the Book of Revelation tells us, the spectre of famine walks the streets.

THE END, THE BEGINNING, OR THE TIME OF CYCLIC RETURN?

How, then, should we understand apocalyptic time? Clearly we are in a field of great tensions. As Catherine Keller writes, 'Time comes tense, edgy, rimmed by tragedy, edged by all our deaths . . .'[15] It has become customary in Christianity to speak of the tension between *chronos* time and *kairos* time, the former being the rhythm of ordinary life, the latter being special time, when, it seems, time stands still, when, as T. S. Eliot wrote, there is 'intensity burning in every moment'.[16] We speak of cyclic time, the time of endless return of the same, in a negative way, but of the rebirth of nature, and our own living out of the rhythm of birth and death, in a positive way. We speak of saving time, marking time, filling in time, killing time (a dreadful phrase), and even worse, mastering time, the control of time. As Emily Dickinson, the nineteenth-century American poet, writes:

'Tis Kingdoms – afterward – they say –
In perfect – pauseless Monarchy –
Whose Prince – is Son of None –
Himself – His Dateless Dynasty –
Himself – Himself diversify –
In Duplicate divine[17]

We have here in a nutshell the politics of patriarchal time, the colonisation of time by the conquerors, the commodification of time by the market. Time loses all its space and embodiment in the cosmos. Instead of the hands of the clock, we have the 'electronic blips of digital time' (Keller, p. 118). For colonisation and the inexorable march of modernity meant not only redrawing the map in Eurocentric colours, but measuring time in western linear terms, in terms of progress and the triumph of reason, the mind over materiality and body. Think of the key dates we learnt: 1492 represents the expansion of Europe into the 'New World' (new in whose terms?); the age of Faith becomes the age of Reason and then the age of Science. And in our own age, we have reinvented space as cyberspace, so that embodiment and cosmic relevance are one degree further removed. Charles Maier speaks of time in the nineteenth century serving as a political instrument forged to 'adjust human life more rationally to the constraints of time and place'.[18] Men in factories have to 'clock in' and 'clock out', so that we now see the creation of public and private time. Small wonder that the sacred clowns of the Pueblo Indians would use alarm clocks in their dances to ridicule 'whites' enslavement to the marching minute hand'.[19]

It can be no coincidence that the Victorian era also invented the idea that woman, 'the angel in the house', had no share in public time, her domestic role trivialised in the time constructs of modernity. Women, in these gender dualisms, represent place, space, Mother Earth, and not time. In this culture/nature split, culture has lost touch with time rooted in place, where the chronology of trees still follow their ancient rhythms. What does time mean for the giant redwood, the mighty oak? Gestation, birth processes – for both animal and human – have their own time, and the sadness is that we have stepped 'out of time' to many of these rhythms. We limp rather than dance to the music of time, or are deaf to its rhythms. Outside my house as I write, a swan sits on her nest on an island in the river. As I rush to work and return, I find her still sitting. I even feel irritated at the calm sense of timefulness she emanates, in contrast with my frequent sense of futile busy-ness.

Yet, thankfully, I know that alongside the fever and fret of daily routine, mythic time lures us into a different experience. In mythic time in all religions we step into the narratives of beginnings and endings. And in terms of Christian faith, the event of incarnation represents the decisive nodal point of time. The Christian midnight (*Minuit Chrétien* as the lovely French carol sings it), the flesh-taking of the Word, brought the spiritual meaning of Resurrection time, time embodied in the mystery of the dying/rising of Christ as eternal now; but in the expectation of the early return of the risen Christ we see the beginnings of apocalyptic time, and the tensions of the repeating of desire and deferral of the end. This, too, would be hijacked by the politics of time, as the Christo-centrism of the Roman Empire imposed the new calendar of BC and AD on the western world (now, of course, changed to BCE/CE, in this pluralist culture). For the Jewish faith, messianic times are the definitive category. The experience of redemption in the messianic moment is what constitutes hope.[20] Israel waits on the Lord, in whom there is plentiful redemption . . .

But apocalyptic time is, by contrast, time at the edges, time confronted by the threat of its own destruction. As Emily Dickinson, the American poet, wrote in the same poem cited earlier:

> Behind Me – dips Eternity
> Before Me – Immortality –
> Myself – the Term between
> Death but the Dawn of Eastern Gray,
> Dissolving into Dawn away
> Before the West begin – [21]

This is precisely the tension of apocalyptic hope. This coming together of time and place here and now, this context in which we are all drawn into a nexus of relating for such a brief moment – how does it fit with the grand scheme of things? How does it fit with the hope of the coming Kingdom, when justice shall reign, and the Second Coming of Christ? With dreams of Utopia? Should we take to the mountains, as the Adventists and many other millennial sects have done, in expectation of the imminent coming, whose horizon is but delayed, and endlessly reinterpreted? Or should we deny all urgency to the apocalyptic warning, and continue fiddling while the planet burns, consuming, spending, laying waste, believing in the endless supply of resources?

That is certainly one response – the anti-apocalyptic one, where the new heaven and the new earth are assumed to be beyond this one. The deadly message conveyed here is that ultimately this earth does not matter. Paradise lies far beyond. Destroy this earth and 'Daddy will give us a new one'.[22]

But there is a third possibility. Keller calls this the counter-apocalyptic stance. 'Counter-apocalypse', she writes, 'would engage the fiery vision of the signifying text and the significance of the contemporary view of burning forests.'[23] If it is true that we live the text of apocalypse, that we cannot avoid enacting it one way or another, then the urgency is to test the way the text is working in our lives. Does Apocalypse actually defer all hope? Does it say Utopias are for when the Kingdom comes? Or is there a possibility of historicising and embodying our hopes, seeing in the graced actions of ordinary people the hope of the coming Kingdom and the hope of the fullness of messianic times, as has been the traditional Christian belief?

There is, of course, a strand running right through our history that hope would be grounded in history in this way. But we have to tease it gently away from other strands which defer all our hope until the end-times. First, let us remove some obstacles. Let us admit the constructed notion of time.

Let us recognise the double strand of our tradition: one dates from Augustine, who constructed the City of God ultimately beyond history; yet there is another strand, emerging first from the monk of Messina, Joachim of Fiore. It happened in the winter of 1190–91 that the English king, Richard the Lionheart, crusader and 'self-styled apocalyptic warrior' (Keller) was about to attack the Muslim leader Saladin, in Jerusalem. Richard identified Saladin as Antichrist, thus justifying his adventures of slaughter in Europe. Joachim was summoned down the mountains of Calabria to foretell victory for the apocalyptic hero. The crucial importance of Joachim for my story is not so much what he said, namely that Saladin was the sixth dragon, and that there was one more to come; it was more that Joachim offered to him and to us a whole vision of God's plan for history: he gave us something to hope for in history, and the way we can now work for the embodiment of hope in history has much to thank him for.

Joachim speaks in a kind of revolutionary Trinitarianism: this third age is one of liberty, of contemplation, of love, of friends and of children. And we know that there was a working out of this in history, with the rise of the prophetic mendicant movements like the Franciscans, and movements of the free spirit in which women, too, acquired voices – I think of the Beguines and of the prophetic voice of Hildegarde of Bingen, who said, of the end of the world, 'It will be brought forth with gentle words – just as the words of this book are – in the seventh day of quietness.'[24] On and on through history, revolutions and counter-revolutions have enacted the text of apocalypse, and religious movements to the right and left have used the motif of deferral of the end to preach their gospel.[25]

It is interesting that this same following through of the apocalyptic motif of prophesying Christ's victory over the forces of evil and the Second Coming in history has been chosen as a way of heralding the millennium today. *The Times*, on 21 November 1998, announced that Botticelli's *Mystic Nativity*, in the National Gallery, is to be a centrepiece of the Gallery's millennium celebration. The *Mystic Nativity* was painted to celebrate the half millennium in 1500, and is widely thought to be influenced by the fiery preaching of the reforming Dominican friar Savonarola who had been executed in 1498. As always with the theme of apocalypse, here Italy's troubles – foreign invaders, disease and conflict – are said to herald 'end-times', but here, not merely 'end-times' but 'the dawning of the half-time after the time', or the half millennium.[26] The organiser of the Exhibition, Carol Plazotta, says that Botticelli's sentiments matched the intermingled emotions of the time – fear, hope, hysteria. 'He [Savonarola] linked the French invasion of Italy in 1494 to the coming apocalypse. To ensure Florence's salvation he stressed avoiding worldly excess, lighting the original Bonfire of Vanities.'[27] Reflecting this, Botticelli has painted the Virgin less sensually than women in his earlier works, and the Magi and the shepherds wear the same sober clothing. In addition, there are quotations from a prayer by Savonarola to the Virgin. The whole scene conveys the time of peace which the Second Coming will bring.

But instead of reading history through this lens of apocalypse – even through the liberating strand represented by Moltmann, Keller and others – I suggest that a more liberating way of historicising hope is offered by Isaiah. First, the messianic hopes he announces are to be realised in history. There is every reason to believe that child whose birth he hopes for in Isaiah 7:13–16, the child who knows how to refuse evil and do good, will be the King's son. (I realise that Christian understanding would see the *sensus plenior* of this text as referring to Jesus.) The fact that King Ahaz would not listen and obey Isaiah was a source of great grief to the prophet, and he binds up his testimony and seals his scroll (8:16). The next time the child is spoken of – the Wonderful Counsellor,

Mighty God, Prince of Peace – it is in much more directly messianic terms. Ahaz, the worldly king, has failed. Isaiah, who received a prophetic call directly in front of the throne of God (Isaiah 6), now sees Yahweh as true king. This messianic child will receive authority directly from God. This I will develop in Chapter 2, where we have the great vision of messianic peace, where domestic animals are in harmony with wild ones and where the remnant of faithful people are the true Israel.

The point is that this is a hope earthed in history: and it is based not on a mighty conflict between good and evil, but on obedience to God's will, a discernment of this in history, and a right sense of timeliness, waiting till the time is right. Isaiah never leaves his people in desolation. Even after the most terrible predictions of the devastated earth, the following chapter offers us the messianic banquet on Mount Zion (a text well-loved in funerals), where not only will there be 'a feast of rich food, a feast of well-aged wines', but 'the Lord God will wipe away the tears from all faces' (25:8). Following on that, Isaiah 35 predicts that

> . . . the eyes of the blind shall be opened
>   and the ears of the deaf unstopped . . .
> For waters shall break forth in the wilderness,
>   and streams in the desert.
>
> (Isaiah 35:5, 6b)

In the coupling of the healing of people and healing of earth, Isaiah gives the basis of a spirituality of hope. And, having looked at the fundamental character of hope, the hijacking of time in history to follow political agendas of conquest and dominance, I now ask, in the final section of this chapter, what all this says to us for spirituality today.

Since, in this stressed state, we have run out of time; and since, in the earth's devastated condition, she too has run out of time, how to recover a proper sense of time is the question. The first way is a reconversion to the earth and to her ecological rhythms. The American poet Adrienne Rich, in her great poem 'The Spirit of Place', roots time firmly in the earth's seasons:

> The work of winter starts fermenting in my head
> how with the hands of a lover or a midwife
> to hold back till the time is right
>
> force nothing, be unforced
> accept no giant miracles of growth
> by counterfeit light
>
> trust roots, allow the days to shrink
> give credence to these slender means
> wait without sadness and with grave impatience
>
> here in the north where winter has a meaning
> where the heaped colors suddenly go ashen
> where nothing is promised
>
> learn what an underground journey
> has been, might have to be; speak in a winter code
> let fog, sleet, translate; wind, carry them.[28]

Perhaps the language of unregulated capitalism at this late stage cannot learn this language of growth according to the seasons, trust in the hidden growth of roots; the slow maturing invisible to the naked eye. Sadly, growth is now measured solely in terms of profit, as expansion of the economy without inflation. But Isaiah discerns the truth of ecological wisdom and links it with the crisis that beset eighth-century Judah:

Therefore my people go into exile without knowledge;
their nobles are dying of hunger
  and their multitude is parched with thirst.

(Isaiah 5:13)

What kind of knowledge does Isaiah mean?[29] In the context of a spirituality which attends to time, it is the lost connections between natural rhythms and human lifestyle that are being sought. We need to get our hands and feet back into the soil in practical ways, know the connection between growing food and cooking and eating it; know which plants grow in each season and which are natural to our own bio-region. It is not necessary either for our salvation or our happiness that we have the immense range of products from the entire world the whole year long, in and out of season, in our supermarkets.

But at the same time, as the late May Sarton wrote, we need to be 'Gardeners of the Spirit':

> Help us to be the always hopeful
> Gardeners of the Spirit
> Who know that without darkness
> Nothing comes to birth
> As without light
> Nothing flowers.[30]

This idea of tending, attending to time, takes us into the spirituality of paying attention, of watching and waiting. This was famously expressed by such writers as Iris Murdoch, Simone Weil, and T. S. Eliot's 'wait without hope/For hope would be hope for the wrong thing'[31] and throws into relief the question of justice in relation to a spirituality of hope.

This is the problem faced by the German feminist theologian Christina Thürmer-Rohr: she associates hope with the aggression of conquest, the 'young white man's idealist venture to the new frontier, or the old white man's yearning for immortality'.[32] To counteract this aggressive optimism, she

---

proposes a stance of living 'hope-lessly in the present'. Yet – and this point is also made by Keller – hope, apocalyptic hope, is strongest in slave cultures and essential for the energy to keep the struggle for survival going – as the next chapter will explore. The point is always to ground hope in a matrix of possibilities for wholeness and growth. And attentive to what the rhythm of time as *kairos* time might mean, neither 'the best of times' nor 'the worst of times',[33] but *the right time*, the aim is to discover what Christ meant by the *now* of salvation, the moment of Enlightenment for the Buddha.

But that is exactly the question: what is the horizon or field of possibilities for us? For Isaiah it was discerning the will of God in history, as opposed to that of weak, secular kings; and in the reworking of the earlier texts, Isaiah 61 makes it crystal clear that it is for the most broken-hearted, vulnerable and the poorest that the Good News is preached. This means that when the young Jesus of Nazareth proclaims the same prophetic text in the synagogue at the beginning of his ministry (Luke 4:18) it is particularly to broken people that hope is offered; and it is offered now, in the possibilities and limitations of the present moment. It is offered to people for whom there is no tomorrow, people like the Salvadorean poet of resistance, Matilda Elena Lopez, for whom there is no future:

> I cry in the cocoon
> for the wings of tomorrow
> the future is a tortured today
> that doesn't yet have wings.[34]

What Jesus offers as *kairos*, the jubilee tradition of cancellation of debts, freeing slaves, and liberating the land, *this* is the great hope for the new millennium, as the Jubilee 2000 campaign proclaims. In fact, it is a challenge requiring commitment on both micro and macro levels.

From out of the chaos of fragmentation, the isolation of

illness and disability, the lack of a future, a spirituality of hope moulds and shapes whatever will keep the flickering candle burning. It may be that the grand dream does not materialise yet; as Isaiah and his followers grew to understand, the constant reshaping of hope in new situations was the prophetic task. It may be that there is not an end to darkness, only a way of seeing in the dark, only lighting a candle within it. But that is why we keep the feast, in ceremonial time, Sabbath time, mythic time, the time of telling the stories that give substance to our hope.

I end this chapter with another image. This time it is the children of the project Wells for India, in a desert area of Rajasthan (see Illus. 1).[35] These are the children of local prostitutes, some kidnapped from many parts of India. The chances of their growing to adulthood without being sucked into prostitution are slim. But these children are full of life, have dreams of being doctors and lawyers and teachers, and the name of the project is Asha – the Hindi word for *hope*. They remind us of the words of a contemporary Israeli poet:

> Darkness is not all,
> Nor war the last word;
> not by a long shot, or a short.
> The children speak it;
> the last word. Hope.
> Hope; the children.
> The child.[36]

Children as bringers of hope are a vibrant witness to the words of the Brazilian liberation theologian, Leonardo Boff:

> As attested to by all the cultures and civilisations the world has known there is a principle of hope at work wherever people have lived that generates great excitement and utopian visions in spite of the fact that of the 3,400 years

of recorded human history 3,166 were years of war, and the remaining 234 were years of preparing for war.[37]

With this as our history, hope cannot be anything else but outrageous. Can we redeem this time with the quality of our hope? That is the question being explored in this book.

CRYING FREEDOM WHEN THE DREAM HAS DIED: SUBVERSIVE TEXTS AND THE STRUGGLE FOR SURVIVAL

INTRODUCTION

'Crying Freedom!' – that great motivating cry blowing through history, from the pleading of the children of Israel in slavery in Egypt to the freedom struggles in all parts of the world, like South Africa, and the memories of the many who, like Steve Biko, died for the dream of freedom; this cry introduces the theme of Chapter 2, how to keep hope alive when the dream has died. If the first chapter prepared the way by asking how to attend to time at this moment in history, the golden thread of the pursuit of hope leads us to explore whether there is a dream, a discourse of freedom for this specific time/space and interweaving of many cultures.

First, a few examples to highlight this theme. Anne Paton, widow of Alan Paton, who wrote *Cry, the Beloved Country*[1] while grieving that her husband died before Nelson Mandela's release from prison, has now, reluctantly, left South Africa, describing this in a very public way as the need to 'Fly the Beloved Country': her experience of freedom did not match up to the dream of life beyond apartheid.[2] On the other side of the Atlantic, Daniel Ortega, formerly President of

Nicaragua in the rosy, idealist days of the Sandinista government – the government of those who overthrew the dictator
Somoza – is now a fallen hero, as this country (one of the
tragic victims of the recent Hurricane Mitch), following
the failure of the Sandinista government, has been gradually
seduced by the lure of global capitalism.

The third example more directly touches European society.
In 1990, while in Britain we were celebrating the fall of
communism and the so-called liberation of East Germany, at
the Ecumenical Congress of European Christian women in
York, some East German women presented participants with
a mime, depicting how they saw themselves: they wandered
in the wilderness, the socialist dream dead, but with no beck-
oning Promised Land, no vision, no hope. All they saw being
offered to them were the alluring arms of western capitalism.

This is precisely the theme of the pursuit, the odyssey, of
hope: how to sustain hope when the dream has died. First, I
explore how the theme of exile formed the context for Isaiah's
discourse of hope, when the Jewish people were defeated by
the Babylonians, and carried off to exile in Babylon. Second,
I ask how the theme of exile characterises our own situation. I then move into a deeper reflection on Isaiah's
subversive strategies, asking what this means for the prophet's
own experience of God. Finally, I bring all this together in a
spirituality of hope, focused through the evocative phrase,
'Resistance is the secret of joy'.[3]

DEATH OF A DREAM

The media ensure that there can be no feigning of ignorance
of the social consequences of exile. Television screens have
been filled for the last ten years (at least) with the most terrible
exoduses from many parts of Africa, due to drought, or bitter
conflict, sometimes civil war, sometimes invasions. No one

can forget the floods of refugees from Rwanda fleeing the Hutu, then the reprisals by the Tutsi and counter-exodus of the former tribe. Nor can the sight of vast numbers of starving people on the move from Sudan in search of the emergency feeding camps ever be forgotten. At the time of writing, we are witnessing, nightly, the unending traumatised floods of refugees from Kosovo, fleeing the Serbian troops in terror, to join those already living in camps. At the same time it is easy to blot out from consciousness the continued existence of the Palestinian camps; like a festering wound, they are a constant reminder that there are many who are 'exiles in their own land'. And of course, this situation of being 'exiles in their own land' can be applied to many indigenous people the world over.

What, then, do we find as we revisit Babylon of the sixth century BCE – a city and civilisation in what is now known as Iraq? It is difficult – almost impossible – to get a realistic glimpse of an ancient culture, flourishing since the beginning of the second millennium before Christ, as now, inevitably, Christianity sees Babylon through the apocalyptic condemnations of the Revelation to John: the text is well known:

Fallen, fallen is Babylon the great!
  It has become a dwelling place of demons,
a haunt of every foul spirit . . .
For all the nations have drunk
  of the wine of the wrath of her fornication.

(Revelation 18:2a, 3a)

This dramatic account of Babylon's fall is in line with the measure of her grandeur. For it was in Babylon that the Tower of Babel stood, symbol of vaulting ambition, as well as the gigantic Temple of Marduk and the great Hanging Gardens. And of course Babylon was well lit at night, since the Babylonians had already learnt how to extract petroleum from the ground. And 'below this temple Babylon lay spread out, a city of broad thoroughfares and narrow lanes, of rubbish-strewn streets, of foetid smells mingled with the scent of myrrh, of noise and bustle, a city boasting bazaars and a sacred avenue flanked by one hundred and twenty brazen lions.'[4]

Such was the setting for the ministry of the prophet we call Second Isaiah. In comparison with the contemporary tragedies of refugees and exiles cited earlier, the Jews were not badly treated in Babylon. The evidence seems to show that most of them settled down to normal life, became assimilated and thus the focus of their identity was weakened. I dare to suggest setting aside the traditional assumption that Second Isaiah (Chapters 40—55) is a book that stands alone. I think we have to understand the work of the prophet here in the light of the messianic promises of the earlier texts, his belief in the hope-filled future of the House of David and Yahweh's promise of peace among the nations.[5] Hence I continue to refer to the writer of these chapters as Isaiah.

Exile in Isaiah's terms was desolation, loss of a homeland, and above all, loss of identity. The Jewish focus of faith, the Temple and the House of David, was destroyed. The monarchy was finished. And the glamour of Babylon was seducing the people from the true God of Israel. Like the story of the East German women in the wilderness, their dream was dead.

And what of contemporary western culture at this *fin-de-siècle* time? Can 'exile in Babylon' function as a metaphor, both critical and disturbing, without trapping us with the sense of 'no exit' referred to in the previous chapter? Without wanting to lose the force of the situation of actual exiles in our midst and elsewhere, and their unjust expulsion from land and home, I suggest this is a very apt motif. In this culture of rampant individualism, where the golden calf of money is worshipped, where the media bombard us with pressures to 'shop till we drop', the motif of being in exile seems very appropriate. 'How shall we sing the Lord's song?' is exactly the question when the culture of the Beast, and a globalised, unchecked capitalism tramples on the poor exactly as was happening in the time of Isaiah. Part of the problem is that the churches and faith communities, like the Jews in Babylon are too easily assimilated to such a culture. Perhaps another Confessing Church is needed, a Church of the faithful remnant, as in the days of Dietrich Bonhoeffer under Nazism, to witness to prophetic truth.

Let us first revisit Isaiah's attempts to keep alive the dream.

SUBVERSIVE STRATEGIES

How does the prophet rekindle his people's hope — a hope, not only *not* outrageous, but long lost sight of? I invite the reader, first, to enter into a strategy of reading *against* the grain of the text as we have it — to become subversive readers of the text, in other words. This has long been a strategy in feminist readings of the Bible, to tease out and uncover hidden meanings of the text, often using sources outside the Bible. For example, the New Testament says nothing about the work of fisher*women*, and much about the work of fisher*men*. Yet, anyone who comes from a fishing community, like Grimsby, or my own Northumberland, knows that women mend the nets, and are involved in the work of cleaning, gutting and marketing of fish. In Tamil Nadu (India), the women do everything except catch the fish — they are considered to be polluted and forbidden to enter the sea. (A bizarre exception — to a western understanding — is that if you are Christian women, you may do so on Christmas Day.[6]) This knowledge causes a certain amount of suspicion as regards certain texts, urging us to ask different questions of them.

What Isaiah is doing is fighting a culture of assimilation and urging his people to put Babylon itself under suspicion. As Walter Brueggeman so poignantly wrote: 'Babylon is to be resisted: it will destroy the soul of Israel!'[7] I will use the example of food to show this, and then proceed to see how Isaiah even subverts the people's understanding of God to reawaken hope in the steadfastness of Yahweh. For it is to Second Isaiah that we look for an evocative poetic description – this prophet is also a brilliant poet – drawing us into the *mystery of the otherness of God*. Let us hear again those famous lines of Isaiah 55:

> Ho, everyone who thirsts,
>   come to the waters,
> and you that have no money,
>   come, buy and eat!
> Come, buy wine and milk
>   without money and without price.
> Why do you spend your money for that which is not
>   bread,
>   and your labour for that which does not satisfy?

How should these lines be understood? It is tempting to see them as a call to the poverty-stricken, an offer of free food: 'Look, benefits exist even here in Babylon!' Yet this should be resisted. A favourite feminist interpretation is to see this as a Wisdom text, a text of the female divine figure, Hokmah/ Sophia (who will be encountered later in this book), who sets her table and invites the poor and vulnerable to eat. I do not discard this meaning completely. But, as I have said, many Jews were quite comfortable in Babylon – in fact those who stayed behind in Judah on their subsistence strips of land perhaps had a worse time.

There is another way, which is to see in this text the *subversive use of food*. This I will make the basis of my spirituality of resistance, 'Resistance is the secret of joy'. Walter Brueggeman suggests that Isaiah is saying to us, 'Don't eat the food of Babylon, don't drink the wine, refuse the excesses; don't be seduced by the demoralising culture.' For the God of Israel offers you food and drink.

Next, I invite you to think of the story in the Book of Daniel (Chapter 1) which also describes the decadence of the Babylonian court. Here Daniel and three other noble young men of Israel, 'endowed with knowledge and insight', are brought to King Nebuchadnezzar's palace to serve the king. They are to be allowed wine and rations from the palace. But Daniel refused such defilement and would only accept vegetables and water. When the palace-master demurred, afraid that the king would punish him if Daniel and his group were in poor condition compared with the rest, Daniel begged for an experiment of ten days. At the end of this time, Daniel and the three were all found to look fitter and fatter than the others. 'God gave knowledge and skill in every aspect of literature and wisdom; Daniel also had insight into all visions and dreams' (Daniel 1:17). Again, what is seen is the subversive use of food *as protest* against the oppression of Babylon. Resistance in this way also cuts through the facile division into victim and oppressor. The victim, too, *cries freedom*, and in activating a culture of resistance, keeps hope alive.

But what a basis is found here for a eucharistic theology of hope. It leads us right to the action of Jesus, filled with hope for the coming Kingdom, who, in Mark 14, takes the cup and says, 'Truly I tell you, I will never again drink of the fruit of the vine until that day when I drink it new in the kingdom of God' (14:25).

Because Isaiah uses the basic symbols of sustenance, as Jesus in his parables did also, *he highlights the counter-culture that God offers in opposition to the excess and decadence of Babylon.* Two contemporary examples will be given of the continuing power of such subversive symbolism. First, the liberation feminist theologian Chung Hyun Kyung, in her keynote speech at an international gathering of women theologians in Costa Rica, on the subject of 'Women Resisting Violence: Towards a Spirituality of Life', told the story of Soo Bock, a poor Korean woman, married off at fourteen years to a leper, from whom she ran away. She was eventually captured by Japanese soldiers during the Second World War and became a so-called comfort woman for them. I refrain from giving the details of the degradation and suffering this meant for Soo Bock. Many of these women died from starvation, exhaustion or from the injuries that resulted from wounds at their brutal treatment by these soldiers.

The point of telling you this story is that Soo Bock chose to survive and *began to eat* and to be obedient. Eating was a choice to survive and to make hope possible. In the end Soo Bock did escape to Thailand, married a Chinese man, and actually experienced some love in her life.[8] This kind of theme features again and again in 'cry freedom' contexts. A second example is Alicia Partnoy, who disappeared in Argentina, was imprisoned, reappeared, was reimprisoned and then went into exile: her poetry reveals how the body is a battleground on which the torturers struggle to gain control over the whole human person. Hence the real significance of bread in keeping hope alive:

> Bread is . . . a means of communicating, a way of telling the person next to me: 'I'm here. I care for you. I want to share the only possession I have.' Sometimes it is easy to convey the message . . . sometimes it is more difficult; but when the hunger hits, the brain becomes sharper. The blanket on the top bed (of a bunk bed) is made into a kind of stage curtain that covers the wall, and behind the curtain, pieces of bread go up and down at the will of stomachs and hearts.
>
> When tedium mixes with hunger, and four claws of anxiety pierce the pits of our stomachs, eating a piece of bread, very slowly, fibre by fibre, is our great relief. When we feel our isolation growing, the world we seek vanishing in the shadows, to give a brother [or sister] some bread is a reminder that true values are still alive.[9]

There are many such stories – of prisoners, of hostages, from the camps, from Auschwitz. These two focus specifically on the link between bread and hope. For exiles, eating the bread of home keeps the dream of return alive, as Rigoberta Menchu, the Guatemalan activist and Nobel prize winner related, when she made tortillas (basic food for a Guatemalan) in her Paris apartment.[10]

Thus the bread and wine offered by Second Isaiah represents not only the physical needs of the people, but his struggle for the soul of Israel. The theme of the alternative culture proposed by God is contained in the prophet's many assertions that

> my thoughts are not your thoughts,
> nor are your ways my ways, says the Lord.
>
> (Isaiah 55:8)

A wonderfully imaginative poetry now conveys the message to the people. 'All flesh is grass', but God's word endures, God's steadfastness, God's justice and peace are for ever. Isaiah brings them now not condemnation but comfort, consolation and the image of God who feeds God's flock like a shepherd. But that God is *other*, we are left in no doubt. It is clear that God is *other* than the gods of Babylon, for they are finished: as the prophet says, 'Bel bows down, Nebo stoops' (Isaiah 46:1). But also *other* than our expectations. And here is where we need, in our subversive reading, to try not to read out the *otherness* of what the text is telling us. For

> I am the Lord, and there is no other.
> I form light and create darkness,
> I make weal and create woe.
>
> (Isaiah 45:6c, 7a)

How does a theology of hope deal with this? I suggest that as Christians, we are uncomfortable with this language, that we read it out of the text, and consequently, Christianity lacks a robust theology to deal with catastrophe and tragedy. The God of love must have nothing to do with evil, it has frequently been asserted. This is actually a crucial point for Jewish–Christian relations. Consequently, when disaster strikes, hope crumbles, and we complain that God is absent. In fact, the feminist Jewish scholar Judith Plaskow has challenged Christianity as being the only religion refusing to look at the darkness of God.[11] She asserts that when God proclaims, through Isaiah, 'I make weal and create woe', 'he is speaking out of the inclusive understanding of monotheism as embracing the totality of experience.'[12]

Let us stay with this otherness. What Isaiah is now doing is recalling the people to remember that 'you are memory of the people of the covenant' and doing it through the motif that God the Creator is Israel's husband – 'your Maker is your husband' (54:5). In other words, he is awakening what the liberation theologians call 'dangerous memory', the memory of the past as critique of the present. Remember, says the prophet,

> . . . the Lord has called you
> > like a wife forsaken and grieved in spirit,
> like the wife of man's youth when she is cast off,
> > says your God.
> For a brief moment I abandoned you,
> > but with great compassion I will gather you.
> In overflowing wrath for a moment
> > I hid my face from you,
> but with everlasting love I will have compassion on you,
> > says the Lord, your Redeemer.
>
> > > (Isaiah 54:6–8)

Again I am shaken by the difficulties of the sheer otherness of these words: the anger of God; the idea of God's casting off of Israel like a man divorcing a wife for a younger woman. When I think of the social setting behind the reference to the 'casting off the wife of one's youth', namely, the vulnerability of young women, of widows, then and now, still, in many cultures of the world; when I also recall that these words are being addressed to people dwelling in Babylon, where the degrading practice of temple prostitution was mandatory for young girls (who couldn't even get married before they had serviced someone in the Temple), I am confronted with the otherness of this God and have to recognise that at a certain level Isaiah, like all the prophets, is insensitive to the vulnerable social context for women.

Faced with the fact of God's wrath, the divine anger, even 'for one brief moment', it becomes easy to recognise why Christian theologians are accustomed to reading out of the text any connection of the divine with anger or vindictiveness, and have labelled this as 'the Jewish view of God'. The Japanese theologian Kazoh Kitamori has called this wrath of God the other side of the coin to the pain and sorrow of God.[13] But now, both anger, sorrow and love are brought together by the compassion of God with which the passage ends.

Despite what I have just said about his sociological insensitivity, it is to Isaiah that we look for the most beautiful expression of womb-like compassion, *rehem*, *rahamim*, with which the prophet expresses the mothering dimension of God.

> Can a woman forget her nursing child,
> > or show no compassion for the child of her womb?
> Even these may forget,
> > Yet I will not forget you.
>
> > > (Isaiah 49:15)

Could this be saying something crucial about the prophet's own understanding of God? But how, then, is the otherness of this compassionate mothering God to be understood? The context says: if God is mother, then this motherhood is part of the otherness and mystery of God. At this time of social upheaval, in a culture where temple prostitution is the norm, positive female images are here used to affirm women previously excluded. This is not a retreat to the domestic scene, as is sometimes assumed when mothering images are used, but offers a new possibility of women's more public role. But the fact that God is both creator *and* husband means that there should be no recourse to simplistic gender stereotyping: making, creating and compassionate mothering are not opposed to the role of a husband!

Within this sense of compassionate mothering the people are reminded of the covenant with Noah. First Abraham and Sarah were remembered: 'Sing, O barren one who did not bear!' And then we are drawn even further back to a more ancient memory when God promised that the waters would never destroy the earth again. But here there is an additional promise:

> For the mountains may depart
>   and the hills be removed,
> but my steadfast love shall not depart from you,
>   and my covenant of peace shall not be removed,
>   says the Lord, who has compassion on you.
>
> (Isaiah 54:10)

What is this covenant of peace? Surely this notion draws us deep into the mystery of God and the prophet's own, deep, mystical experience of this; because we have stayed with the painful process through anger, the withdrawal of God, the suffering of the forsaken wife, but then a renewal of mothering compassion, we can hear more; by staying with these tensions we are drawn back into the original covenant with Noah to receive a new promise of a mystical vision of peace and harmony which is characteristic of the yearning of this great prophet/poet.

Splendour upon splendour is heaped on the people, whose

city will be set with rubies, and its gates with jewels (v. 11). Not the pedagogy of Babylon, but God will be their teacher, educating them in righteousness. But then comes the paradox – remember that we are still struggling with the tension of 'I make weal and create woe', and God's involvement with the evil of creation:

> If anyone stirs up strife,
>> it is not from me.

(Isaiah 54:15a)

I think we are plunged deep into the mystery of creation here. Somehow God takes responsibility for weal and woe. But no one should see this as licence to choose evil, death and destruction. This text comes up with a different answer to the strangeness of God. Yes, says God, I created the smith who blows the fire of coals, and makes the weapons of destruction. Yes, I created the ravager to destroy (v. 16) and, yes, the message, 'No weapon that is fashioned against you shall prosper', is as difficult now as it was then.

Has God just failed? After all, the people had been defeated, carried off to captivity, and their dream had died. The bombs fashioned now are killing the innocents all over the world – Belgrade, East Timor and the Sudan. All we can do, says Isaiah, is to remember that the ancient promises of God fashion the very possibility of life and death. Stay with the faithfulness and the compassion of God. Feminist spirituality will add: stay also with the vulnerability of the mothering God. This God who offers the vision of peace seems to be at home with the reality of suffering. As someone suffering from AIDS wrote recently: 'Auschwitz makes no sense. AIDS makes no sense. We just end up standing stunned by the awful (awe-filled?) horror of it all. I am beginning to suspect that God is not so much where there is love but where there is suffering.'[14]

With this cry of faith arising out of suffering, let us return from sixth-century Babylon, asking what light is now shed on a spirituality of hope, with its focus as 'resistance is the secret of joy'.

RESISTANCE IS THE SECRET OF JOY

In the first chapter it was suggested that a spirituality of hope should reconvert to a different sense of time, far more attentive to the rhythms of the earth, tending, attending, watching and waiting. Another building block is added to this through the idea that, in so doing, we construct a culture of resistance. As with Isaiah in Babylon, the context of exile is the foundation of this culture of resistance, but 'exile' used here in a positive sense, of resistance to those elements of the twentieth-century culture of global capitalism that are in direct opposition to gospel values. The spirituality of the early Church was also characterised by this counter-cultural element, but for many centuries – in fact, since the Emperor Constantine – it has been true that Christians have had the tendency to become too happy in Babylon.

Consider for a moment the many spiritualities that arose as a culture of protest against corruption and abuse of power. In fact, the monastic movements began as a retreat from city to desert, as a counter-cultural protest against the decadence of city life. A spirituality of resistance and struggle refuses to let injustice have the last word. Let us be clear: this is not an opting out from society, a retreat to an inner world where Christians settle down cosily with their own ideals, and give up on social critique. Far from it: prophetic critique today will work as far as possible with whatever forces or energies of society are leading in the right direction. The point about a spirituality of resistance is that *we already live from a different vision*. And this is what is so energising.

Is this not what Isaiah was saying? Even here, in Babylon,

God's vision of harmony and peace, promised so long ago, is a gift especially for the present (although the prophet's own longing was for the homecoming to Sion.) Resistance is a far deeper concept than simply activism. Because, in the depth of our hearts, we have said 'no' to injustice and oppression on a global level, something has been liberated deep within us and in the solidarity of the groups with whom we are in relation. *We can recover our collective soul.*

What, then, are the threads woven into the idea of a spirituality of resistance? The first thread is that of anger. And I take this directly from the scriptural idea of godly anger, the anger which made Jesus drive the animal-sellers and money changers out of the Temple (John 2:13–17). Holy anger is a blazing sense of outrage – this simply should not be! It is an anger, or a passion, that drives to justice and makes it. As Carter Heyward wrote:

> What we in the church must be about, I am convinced, is a return to religion of passion – a way of being in which anything less than spilling over with the Spirit of God is not enough; spilling over with desire to know and do the will of God in our daily work and play.[15]

It is not passivity and apathy that bring about change. Anyone who works with victims of abuse knows that one of the first stages out of their trauma is the awakening of anger. Too long have we – particularly women – been schooled into patience and putting up with injustice. The Beatitudes tell us to hunger and thirst after justice: but part of this hungering is righteous anger against violence, whether military, sexual, economic or ecological, the denial of human rights, and the abuse of power within any institution, even the Church itself. As the ethicist Beverly Harrison stated in her inaugural lecture at Union Theological Seminary, New York:

> Can anyone doubt that the avoidance of anger in popular

Christian piety, reinforced by a long tradition of fear of deep feeling in our body-denying Christian tradition, is a chief reason why the church is such a conservative, stodgy institution? . . . We need to recognize that where the evasion of feeling is widespread, anger does not go away or disappear . . . Anger denied subverts community. Anger expressed directly is a mode of taking the other seriously.[16]

Second – again taking inspiration from Isaiah – resistance springs from the centrality of compassion. This compassion is more than a feeling, or emotion. As we have seen, it is rooted in the mothering, womb-like compassion of God. The Buddhists call it the 'boundless compassion of the Bodhisattva'. Aung San Suu Kyi, under house arrest in Burma because of her resistance to the oppressive regime, speaks of compassion as the very strength that keeps her going. In a recent lecture, where she compares Buddhist compassion with Christian *caritas*, she speaks of it as 'the quivering of the heart in response to others' suffering, the wish to remove painful circumstances from the lives of other beings'.[17]

As Isaiah witnessed, it is the power of divine compassion that refuses to abandon a people, however faithless they may be. It is through compassion, it would seem, a*nd not through might*, that God redeems God's people.[18] Vandana Shiva, the famous Indian Professor of Ecology from Delhi, says that her mother has but one question as she faces the beginning of each day: 'How shall I practise compassion?'[19] The great Abbé Pierre, whose whole life has been poured into changing the lives of the homeless poor and awakening society's conscience about this, when involved in a shipwreck from which he narrowly escaped, and asked what regrets he had about life, answered only that he had not loved his neighbour enough.

But, underpinning and fuelling compassion is the power of 'dangerously remembering'. As I have suggested, this is the dangerous memory of the past, both the memories of freedom and those of oppression, memories often blocked by the political circumstances of our times. For example, when I was living in Brussels, African students came to me and said that they only discovered their history by visiting the African Museum in Tervuren, near Brussels. Memories of suffering have been suppressed through shame, humiliation, and by deliberate obliteration – as I discovered, when I came to work on the theological materials for the Irish Famine.[20] We see this same factor working with the Jews in Babylon, who could not sing when they remembered Sion (Psalm 137). I see it also in the tragic systematic obliteration of Armenian Christian culture in Turkey.[21]

Thus, a spirituality of hope cannot be energised to resist, before the act of dangerously remembering has been undertaken. And this is where the theme of prophetic laments appears. There is no adequate response to remembered sorrow until the grieving has been given free expression. And I mean community-based, responsible and ceremonial grieving, not only the abandoned individual, isolated in grief.

The same dynamic is also present in British history: for example, what response is there to a story like this, which took place in Scotland in 1792, the year of the Clearances, the so-called Year of the Sheep, when the great landowners of the Highlands brought in thousands of sheep and drove off the poor crofters?

> Many a thing I have seen in my own day and generation. Many a thing, O Mary, Mother of the black sorrow! I have seen the townships swept, and the big holdings made of them, the people been driven out of the countryside to the streets of Glasgow and to the wilds of Canada, such of them as did not die of hunger and the plague and smallpox while going across the ocean. I have seen the women putting the children in the carts that were being sent . . . while their husbands lay bound in their pen and were weeping beside

them, without power to give them a helping hand, though there women themselves were crying aloud, and their little children were wailing like to break their hearts.[22]

This story is cited to show that the theme of dangerously remembering is indigenous to our lands too. Being 'exiles in their own land' is thus a motif also for the British Isles. Awareness of our history of dangerous memories, of oppression or of pride, must be an ingredient of every culture of resistance. One more example witnesses to the crucial importance of memory. The aid agencies – speaking here of Christian Aid, CAFOD and CIIR – see it as vital part of their work to assist a people to recover the memories which form a central part of their identities. Thus, CIIR together with the Catholic Church in Guatemala is engaged in the Memory project. Up to 220,000 people had been killed in Guatemala between 1954 (when the first US-backed dictatorship was established) and 1994, when the Clinton administration stopped funding the Guatemalan regime. The Memory project asks what has happened to the children, mothers, friends and neighbours of the dead, and how they can make sense of their loss. Silence, through fear of further violence, seems to be the response. Thus, this project, now in its third year,

> helps people to break their silence, encouraging communi-
> ties to reconstruct their experiences of the war. As part of
> this process it accompanies people as they reclaim the
> physical remains of the dead, many of them buried in
> mass graves, and give them a dignified burial and proper
> mourning.[23]

Ian Linden (secretary of CIIR) speaks of the enormous importance of this project, which helps people who have become so numb with suffering that what happened to them is, literally, unspeakable: 'Until the memory of what had happened in the early 1980s was retrieved, the soul of the community could not begin to be repaired. The massacres of the families by the military had, as it were, stopped time for countless people.'[24]

Yet, the memory of suffering and oppression is only half the story. In a spirituality of resistance hope is energised by memories of freedom, of pride in identity, dreams and homeland. This is what the prophet Micah was referring to, in those great laments where the voice of God cries out, 'O my people, what have I done to you?' This is what sustains indigenous peoples, their land and pride removed by the colonising power. But Isaiah reminds us that this very identity depends on the creative and compassionate power of God. And it is memory that forms the heart of Eucharist. It is the memory of God's liberating power that Jesus chooses as the context of his final meal.

It is thus fitting that this chapter ends with a story of the power of ritual, a story of resistance where hope could only be sustained by ritual. It is the story of Acholdeng, a Dinka woman from the southern Sudan who, starving, had walked with her baby son Rial for four days and three nights to reach an Oxfam feeding centre (see Illus. 2).[25] Once she had had a husband, a cow, a field. But last year, he had died, the crop failed in the terrible droughts, people were dying around her and she had barely eaten for two months. With the baby she set off to look for food. The story of this four-day trek is a terrible one – being turned away from feeding centres, the baby and herself creeping ever nearer to death. When they finally reached the Oxfam centre Rial was barely breathing. He was found to have diarrhoea, to be anaemic and to be suffering from hypothermia and dehydration. Exhausted, mother and son curled up on a blanket and slept. She awoke later and was given more food And then something amazing happened:

Even as babies were dying, one by one they [the mothers] left their children on the mats and joined together in a circle . . . They started singing. It sounded like the tiny bells which the Dinka attach to the horns of their best cattle . . . They sang courting songs, songs of prosperity and hope, songs of praise to the cows they didn't have and to the life they only half had. They clapped. They moved back and forth, pounded the baked earth. Whistled and laughed. It was light in the darkness.

Slowly Acholdeng hobbled over to join them, taking up the rhythms and the dance. In minutes, all those in the centre – assistants, mothers who had been grieving, children and doctors – were dancing and singing. It was a great act of defiance against the rotten climate, the accursed war, the land that wouldn't produce, the armies, the cattle raiders and all the troubles.

And this is the heart of a spirituality of resistance. From Isaiah to present-day Sudan, God is energising *the outrageous pursuit of hope.*

PROPHETIC IMAGINATION AND THE NOURISHING OF EARTH COMMUNITIES

The previous chapter ended with a remarkable story of courage in a desperate situation, but perhaps raised the question as to whether hope can be kept alive in other ways than by resisting: there must be more creative ways to hope than resisting the impasse of the status quo! And the narratives of hoping must include all human beings, struggling to make sense and meaning in life. And it would be impossible to write of hope without exploring the role of imagination. There has been a resurgence of interest in imagination among philosophers – and a few theologians.[1] In the context of the Scriptures Walter Brueggeman leads the way.[2] But not many have made the links between imagination/prophecy and earth community. By earth community I mean the many links between people and place, between human beings and the creatures of sky, sea and soil who form the bio-region in all its richness and neediness. I mean the possibilities and limits of a particular climate which dictate what we can grow and eat in season. This involves all the struggles to sow and harvest the crops to feed the communities of people and animals, the interdependencies involved, the rituals and blessings of sowing and harvesting – perhaps forgotten – and the history and memories of what earth and people have suffered and rejoiced in together.

To begin this reflection, let us consider the inspiring words of the American theologian Maria Harris in a remarkably prophetic book, *Proclaim Jubilee: A Spirituality for the 21st Century*: 'The demand is liberation; the emphasis is connectedness; the corrective is suffering; the power is imagination, and the vocation is *tikkun olam*, the repair of the world.'[3]

First, she asserts 'the demand is liberation' – and Chapter 2 focused on 'Cry freedom' as part of a spirituality of resistance and struggle. Next, 'the emphasis is connectedness' points to the fact that a theology of hope seeking to celebrate a Jubilee, must constantly look for healing connections, between spirit and matter, people and earth, and for the deep-seated links between the sufferings caused by poverty, race, gender and heterosexism. That 'the corrective is suffering' points to what will happen to the innocent who hunger and thirst for the justice of the Kingdom, or the kin-dom, of God; and this will be a focus of the following chapter. Lastly, Harris suggests, the vocation is *'tikkun olam'*: this invites us back to an old Jewish story of creation of the seventeenth-century mystical Jewish theologian, Isaac Luria:

> In the beginning [he says], the Creator of the Universe, deciding to make a world, drew in the divine breath – contracted – in order to make room for the creation coming into being. In this enlarged space, the Creator then set vessels, and into the vessels poured the brilliance of divine light. The light was too brilliant for the vessels, however, and unable to contain it, they shattered all over the universe. Since that time, the work of human beings has been to go about the universe, picking up the shards of creation and trying to mend and transform the vessels by refashioning them in a work called 'the repair of the world'.[4]

Gathering and refashioning the fragments of our broken world[5] – is an evocative way to describe the task of redemption; and this is particularly apposite for a spirituality of hope, reshaping of our ideas of wholeness on the basis of chaos and fragmentation, paying special attention to time. But the focus in this chapter is on the words 'the power is imagination'; the question is what kind of imagination permeates and fuels the outrageous pursuit of hope?

This, I argue, is what links the work of Isaiah with a spirituality of hope for the next millennium. For the work of all the great prophets is work, above all, of imagination, full of promise, movement, dynamism, 'providing space and time for the subversion of order', as the writer David Toolan suggests.[6] Akin to but not completely identical with poetic and sacramental imagination, prophetic imagination refuses the present impasse as inevitable, for 'what *must be* takes priority over what *is*'.[7] The important point is that prophetic imagination, like poetic imagination, is not confined to some private daydream, but is a fully public imagination, belonging to the public domain, inspiring the full range of communities belonging to it to commitment to fuller visions of well-being.[8]

This means a refusal to be trapped in the limits of the injustice of the present, the limits of worldly regimes, but most of all the effects of this on the cultural imagination, on what might be called the stultification of the cultural imaginary or symbolic system. If the symbolic imaginary – the set of symbols controlling our hopes and dreams – is ultimately leading humanity to death, to the acceptance of violence as normal, to war as the only activity to energise a flagging patriotism, it needs to be asked, how could these roots be transformed?

Prophetic imagination, or prophetic dreaming, keeping visions alive (as I developed the theme in my book *Beyond the Dark Night*[9]) is what stimulates diverse groups forming society into becoming a culture of life, a biophilic, life-loving culture, to use an ecological term. It is also an authentic dimension of being and becoming Church. Together with the power of dangerous memory, these two activities are at the heart of a theology of hope. For prophetic imagination *is outrageous* – not merely in dreaming the dream, but in already living out of the dream before it has come to pass, and in embodying this dream in concrete actions.

First, I ask how imagination can be recovered in a society like ours, where it seems to have become irrevocably hijacked and stultified by consumerism; then I look to Isaiah for a vision of flourishing which encompasses all living creatures, both human and earth communities, exploring how this can become integrated into the Church's ecological mission, her ethics, liturgy and Christology. Not that we can simply lift a blueprint from the past and assume it offers quick-fix solutions. In the northern hemisphere at least, this world is not the rural agricultural community that Isaiah knew. His questions seem far from the Euro-American context. Nor have Jewish-Christian biblical traditions always been gender sensitive: the prophetic imagination of the Scriptures, like the whole of our western philosophical tradition, is constructed as if men were the sole subjects of history.

Whereas contemporary feminist biblical scholarship tries to redeem the balance in some respects, it has to be admitted that Isaiah still reflects the prejudices of his time. But I take heart from Elisabeth Schüssler Fiorenza's injunction that the Bible is at the same time both liberating and oppressing.[10]

Three examples clarify this: in the oracle against Egypt, part of the punishment will be that 'the Egyptians will be like women and tremble with fear before the hand that the Lord of Hosts raises against them' (Isaiah 19:16) – a familiar stereotype of women as timid, emotional and fearful. The destruction of Babylon is depicted as the humiliation of the virgin daughter as a prostitute. In fact Isaiah shares the marriage image of prophets like Ezekiel and Hosea where Israel is always the faithless bride and the Lord is the faithful husband: in other words, it is always the woman who is the faithless one. There is also the difficult question of his marriage to the prophetess – is this a form of temple prostitution? Isaiah also represents the figure of Lilith in a monstrous form. Lilith, in Jewish legend, was the first wife of Adam, dismissed from the garden because she refused to obey him. (She probably represents a trace of an early pre-Israelite goddess.[11]) When Isaiah describes the devastation of the earth, turned into wilderness,

> Wildcats shall meet with hyenas,
>   goat-demons shall call out to each other,
> there too Lilith shall repose.

> (Isaiah 34:14)

In other words, the long tradition of demonising women as witches finds also a trace in Isaiah. Why, then, dialogue with this text? I hope to show that one of the reasons for continuing to wrestle is that, despite gender essentialism, Isaiah's prophetic imagination insists on the recovery of the collapsed dream and its contemporary embodiment.

For what other way is there to renew the heart of prophecy than through the task of imagining and dreaming as a basis for action? As the Benedictine prioress Joan Chittister wrote,

> We need to intervene for one another. We need a new world view that puts the old one in a 'new light'. But how? And where will this spirituality of contemplative co-creation come from in this individualistic culture? And in what way can the religious leaders of our time build this bridge from privatised piety to public moral responsibility?[12]

Finally, I will conclude by briefly exploring the implications of *liturgical* imagination for ecclesial and faith communities.

THE COUNTER-WORLD OF EVANGELICAL IMAGINATION

The words are Walter Brueggemann's.[13] They suggest that a spirituality of resistance and struggle cannot come into being, let alone flourish, without a counter-cultural seeing, hearing and yearning emerging from the biblical visions[14] – that is, if they can be liberated from the androcentric and patriarchal presumptions I already referred to. How to awaken this prophetic imagination in minds, hearts and spirits – selves that have become so fragmented by the breakdown of community, where pornographic forms of eros afflict a culture whose very psychic imagination has become diseased – that is exactly the problem. Disneyland, not the Promised Land, now captures the public fantasy; public dreams are for ever more expensive cars and luxurious lifestyles.

Sadly, this hijacking of the public imagination has happened at a time when the great liturgies seem to have lost their power to engage the whole person, body, mind and heart. The cosmologist Brian Swimme recalls the ancient cultures where people gathered their young in caves to tell them stories of being initiated into the mysteries of the universe.[15] This meant not simply passing on information, but initiating young people into a sense of awe, wonder, connectedness and responsibility for the sacredness of existence. Sadly, the caves of revelation today are mostly the darkened sitting rooms where children drink in the seductions of today's advertising prophets of television. Yet if a community keeps alive its power of remembering its origins, it can also be stimulated by its power to remember and to dream dreams.[16] 'Unlike the claims of consumer society,' writes Brueggemann, 'the community operates with a powerful vision, a vision that affirms that the future is not yet finished. God has a powerful intention and resolve to bring us to a wholeness not yet in hand.'[17]

At this point it is appropriate to enter into dialogue with

Isaiah, contemporary questions now being linked with the prophet's own counter-cultural imagination. Right from the beginning of his text as we have it shines a vision that denies the violence of society as part of God's purpose: already in Isaiah 2:4 comes the vision of peace that God offers the people:

> He shall judge between the nations,
>   and shall arbitrate for many peoples;
> they shall beat their swords into ploughshares,
>   and their spears into pruning hooks;
> nation shall not lift up sword against nation,
>   neither shall they learn war any more.

Not only is this dream of messianic peace constantly returned to and reworked throughout the book in the light of events (it even appears in the penultimate chapter 65:25: 'The wolf and the lamb will feed together, and the lion shall eat straw like the ox'), but it has proved a constant inspiration right through history (see Illus. 3). Here is a contemporary midrash of Isaiah 2:4 by a graphic artist, where many scriptural texts and images have been woven together:

> Thus says the Compassionate One: As I parted the Sea of Reeds that you might emerge from my Womb, so now it is you who must widen the narrow passages so that justice and mercy can be reborn. Do not be afraid my Beloved. Go forth into the night and become the light and the outstretched arm. And on the day when all the world is set to the rhythm of my timbrel, dominion and violence will be banished from the land and you will know Me, the One Who Makes Life Holy.[18]

Thus, the Exodus image of liberation is here interwoven with the image of giving birth to justice and peace. The Isaian vision of messianic peace seems here to be a reworking of Genesis 2: Paradise is restored. But we are also given here the beginning of what we can call a female cultural imaginary. God is imaged as female, and justice and mercy are seen as emerging from the womb of God. Here too, the dangerous remembering of God's redemptive action is meant to inspire the contemporary building of a world of justice and peace. And again, there is imagery expressive of God's womb-like compassion. Clearly, this prophet-poet offers us seed corn for developing a counter-cultural female imaginary, as a constructive critique of the psychic numbing which props up militarism and a culture of violence.

Second, the vision of Isaiah is inspirational as the Christian Church tries at this critical time of environmental crisis to recover a mission to become ecologically responsible. Many readers will remember that, at the World Council Assembly that was coterminous with the Earth Summit in Rio in 1992, there was a public commitment made by the churches towards becoming earth-centred communities:

> We dare not deny our role as churches in the crisis which now overwhelms us. We have not spoken the prophetic word ourselves. Indeed we did not even hear it when it was spoken by others of late, including a number of scientists. Much less do we hear the cries of indigenous peoples who have told us for centuries that modernity would foul its own nest and even devour its own children. We need to mourn and repent . . . We plead for forgiveness and pray for a profound change of heart.[19]

Sadly, this commitment to repentance was not followed up to a large degree. (Even the official Graz declaration of the Ecumenical Assembly of 1997 offered no great step forward, although on the level of interaction of ordinary people there was both imagination and commitment.[20]) Nor have the commitments of the Earth Summit produced great change.

The fact is that what the ecologist Gwyn Prins calls 'the death of environmental politics' needs urgent attention.[21] Why does the earth always come bottom of the agenda for social justice? As many ecologists say, the oft-repeated statistics as to dying species, global warming, death of the rainforest and so on cease to shock, and to touch our minds and hearts. This approach simply doesn't work. Churches often see ecological issues as belonging to 'creation' (however that is defined), and not to issues of redemption and social justice. The politics of greed also demand and ensure that we human beings keep our positions of superiority – that is, presumed superiority – towards animals, trees and other resources: to disturb this hierarchy of being would hit at too many aspects of contemporary western lifestyle.

Two other approaches are frequently encountered. One is to view ecological concerns as part of the threat to human security: this forces a kind of response, although based on self-interest. As from the comfort of our sofas we watch pictures of people forced to flee their land because of ecological catastrophes of floods or famine, or the violence of civil war, another category of refugees is created and societies are forced into making a response. Similarly, conflicts arise because of acute scarcity of environmental resources, the so-called 'water-wars'. For example, Gwyn Prins tells us:

> Two hundred and fourteen of the major river basins flow through more than 2 countries. Forty per cent of the world's population depend for water on those 214 major river systems. So it was not difficult for the CIA to prepare a map of environmental 'flash points' which marks the course of the great rivers like the Nile and the Euphrates as permanent candidates in this category.[22]

The third approach, which has overtones of racism or traces of imperialism, links the so-called inability of post-colonial states to govern with the disease risks of a tropical climate, and the threat of overpopulation with environmental crises not far behind. In other words, we almost blame such countries for bringing environmental disasters upon themselves.

Yet, to give a recent example, can the poor people of Honduras and Nicaragua be blamed for the destruction of Hurricane Mitch? Can the people of Bangladesh be blamed for the terrifying floods which regularly destroy their country, floods, as is well known, that are related to deforestation on a massive scale? These approaches – the threats to security, the appeal to self-interest, and the accusation of others' inability to govern properly – hardly provide a principled basis on which to structure responsibility.

Equally clearly, a number of factors, institutional and psychological, coalesce to create this denial. All are inter-connected: green issues do not get politicians elected; global tourism does irreparable damage as yet unfaced; globalisation policies, like the patenting of trees and seeds, seem to occupy an unassailable position. The question becomes, how to find a shared, communal will, shared values, shared responsibility for what the earth means to us and the children of the future. As Prins concludes: 'In the killing fields of ecological stress, shared values and joint political will only arise when there is perceived community of vulnerability.'[23]

This is the reason for invoking here the vision of Isaiah specifically as a vision of *flourishing*, involving people and all earth creatures together in overlapping earth communities of peace. For flourishing is now being discovered as a metaphor invoked by ecologists, philosophers of religion and some feminist theologians alike at this moment.[24] Grace Jantzen suggests that not only does flourishing involve human and non-human communities together in responsibility for culture, but the very word is suggestive of a nurturing culture, one which focuses on birth, growth and creativity. This is distinct from a focus on the *metaphor of salvation* with its association with the Fall, guilt and atonement, which has dominated western tradition. This nucleus of images, she considers, encourages an imaginary of death and violence, because the central salvific act remembered and re-presented in the Eucharist is always the recalling of a violent death.

Have Christians become anaesthetised from the shock value of this? Think of Jill Paton Walsh's story, *Knowledge of Angels*: it is set in medieval times, and tells of the little girl reared by wolves, who became the subject of a philosophical experiment to find out whether knowledge of the existence of the divine was innately human or was taught her by the community.[25] The child was being 'civilised' by a remote convent of nuns, who were forbidden to speak to her of anything to do with religion. One day they found her terrified, sobbing with uncontrollable fear and grief. And the reason? She had been into their chapel which was dominated by a huge crucifix. Christ, bleeding from his wounds, suspended as a perpetual memory to this death, affected her far more than the daily, bloody, kill-to-eat practices of the wolf pack.

This is not to challenge the central place of the dying-resurrection motif at the heart of Christianity of which the iconography of the cross plays a central role: it is simply to explore the metaphor of flourishing as found in Isaiah for its promise of a new cultural imaginary and as an organising core for us to become ecologically responsible communities. This is the link between prophetic imagination and the future of community.

A RESURRECTION STORY FOR THE EARTH

The first resource given by the prophet is a resurrection story inclusive of the earth itself. Although the Resurrection of Christ is at the heart of faith, yet contemporary understandings of resurrection are often individualised, personalised and spiritualised into another, post-mortem world. But Isaiah links the recovery, well-being and flourishing of people and all earth creatures together in joyous celebration *now*. These texts are known and loved:

> The wilderness and the dry land shall be glad,
>> the desert shall rejoice and blossom;
> like the crocus it shall blossom abundantly,
>> and rejoice with joy and singing.

(Isaiah 35:1–2a)

This rejoicing is because the glory of the Lord is filling the earth. (Here it is timely to recall the Jewish legend cited at the beginning of this chapter, that God created by withdrawing and that creation could not bear the brilliance of God.) Then – in a passage to be cited by Jesus of Nazareth in a different time and place – Isaiah continues:

> Then the eyes of the blind shall be opened,
>> and the ears of the deaf unstopped;
> then the lame shall leap like a deer;
>> and the tongue of the speechless sing for joy.
> For waters shall break forth in the wilderness
>> and streams in the desert.

(Isaiah 35:5–6)

The prophetic conviction that the entire creation will be bathed in the newness of resurrection suggests that the focus should not be on the violent evil of the crucifixion, which may suggest that society is forever frozen into inevitable bloodshed – even the wolf child was shocked before the crucifix! Rather, could we imagine the flourishing of earth and people together, in full splendour? This can only happen through commitment to the work of re-creation in full awareness of this broken web of life. *Imagination is no abstract activity but embodied, energising commitment.*

This is an example from my own experience: in the work of our small NGO, Wells for India, in the desert of Rajasthan, our group has been privileged to see what this text could mean[26] – as part of a resurrection story for a desert people.[27] Isaiah's picture of a once-fertile land not only turning to desert but to jungle, haunt of the wild beasts, a place of fear, is for us all too real. When water returns to desert communities – land ravaged through drought, deforestation, and a desperate poverty increased through globalisation policies – the sacramental principle that *water gives life* is seen as the key to the resurrection story. The wellsprings flow again and little children do not die from water-related illnesses; villages come to life as agriculture becomes possible and the men do not flee to the cities – those festering lumps of misery – in search of work. Like the Samaritan woman who came to the well and encountered Jesus, women do not have to set off into the desert in search of water, carrying on their heads up to forty kilogrammes of weight in ceramic water-jars or metal vessels, but come to their own village well and discover new possibilities for health, education and job creation.

And all of this in a culture which, like that of the biblical society, is steeped in faith, faith that water is a gift of God and its new flowing is to be celebrated with thanksgiving, in feast, song and dance. Not for nothing are the wells in this desert region named 'Oceans of Life', 'Channels of Peace', as flourishing becomes a possibility once more, as the spiritual values of justice, mercy and peace are intertwined with material flourishing.

But the second focus is that this vision of flourishing in Isaiah is rooted in what I call *ecological wisdom*. 'My people go into exile for lack of knowledge' (Isaiah 5:13), and of course Isaiah's own passion in the face of the ruined hopes of the people was for the restoration of the Davidic kingship and the rebuilding of the temple. It is by reading his text with an ecological lens that I discover this mourning for a lost wisdom. Again and again the theme of the lack of knowledge is repeated.

'Whom will he teach knowledge,
    and to whom will he explain the message?
Those who are weaned from the milk,
    those taken from the breast?'

(Isaiah 28:9)

From the very passage understood as the call of Isaiah, Isaiah received this terrible, paradoxical command from Yahweh:

'Go and say to this people:
"Keep listening, but do not comprehend;
keep looking but do not understand."
Make the mind of this people dull,
    and stop their ears,
    and shut their eyes,
so that they may not look with their eyes,
    and listen with their ears,
and comprehend with their minds,
    and turn and be healed.'

(Isaiah 6:9–10)

Usually this is taken to mean, *not* that God did not want the people to listen and understand; rather, that Yahweh took into consideration the failure of the prophetic call (this is how the passage is cited in Matthew 13), and the historical fact that people did not begin to repent until after the final destruction.

The prophet's response is significant: He says, 'How long, O Lord?'

'Until cities lie waste,
    without inhabitant,
and houses without people,
    and the land is utterly desolate.'

(Isaiah 6:11)

Here, a link is made with the context of Exodus, where the hardening of Pharaoh's heart prevented the Israelites from

---

1. 'The children speak it; the last word. Hope.' The children of the Asha Project, Rajasthan, India. (Asha is the Hindi word for hope.)
(*Photograph:* Mary Grey.)

2. 'A Dance in the Shadow of Death.' The power of ritual in a spirituality of resistance.
(*Photograph:* © Mike Goldwater/Network.)

3. 'The Peaceable Kingdom' by Edward Hicks shows how the prophetic imagination of Isaiah has been inspirational in a vastly different historical context.

(Philadelphia Museum of Art, Pennsylvania/Bridgeman Art Library, London.)

4. 'Once upon a time there was wisdom
(*Sophia*), and she was present everywhere with all the intensity and all the
desire of all there was. . . .'

('Sophia' by Robert Lentz,
© Robert Lentz, 1991)

5. Jesus learnt from his mother Mary, Daughter of Wisdom (*Sedes Sapientiae*), as she had learnt from her mother, the St Anne of tradition.

(Masaccio and Masolino, 'Madonna and child with St Anne', Galleria degli Uffizi, Florence/Bridgeman Art Library, London.)

6. The Trinity in the form of three rabbits in ceaseless, circular motion is an image suggesting that the entire creation reveals the beauty of God.

(Stained glass window, Holy Trinity Church, Long Melford, Suffolk.)

leaving Egypt, but also made God's glory more manifest at the eventual Passover and crossing of the Sea of Reeds. The theme of re-creation is not far away (especially in the later writing in the so-called Book of Comfort). But my argument is that in this continual tale of destruction, the loss of the northern kingdom, the fall of Samaria, and eventual conquest of Judah, the involvement of ecological catastrophe is interwoven with the fate of the people: the failure of wisdom and fidelity brings down ruin on people and land alike.

It could be retorted that ecological wisdom means one thing for the agricultural society of eighth- and seventh-century Judah, and another thing for today, our context being urban and technological. Yet Isaiah's audience was a city audience, his concern was with the city of Jerusalem, its fate and the possibility of homecoming and reconstruction.

Again, to make a separation between city and countryside is dangerous; this is to assume too easily that ecological concerns are not urban concerns. Of course this is an illusion: as polluted cities become unfit for humans to dwell in them (even to breathe!) in many parts of the world, it is because the villages are unsustainable that poor people flee to the cities. How food is grown (or genetically manipulated), how animals are treated, what poisons are flung into the soil, are concerns for every unit of dwelling. Corporations busy patenting trees and plants, or 'terminator' seeds, so that poor farmers now have to buy fresh seed every year, instead of being able to use the seeds they have saved, present ethical issues for all.

A scene from one of India's cities comes to mind. Once I was in the city of Jaipur, in a nightmare of swirling traffic, rickshaws, bicycles, cars and taxis. Suddenly it appeared to come to a standstill. It was time to feed the cows who wandered into the middle of a busy roundabout. It may have been exasperating, but the rhythm of nature had to be respected.

So it is clear that Isaiah's prophetic knowing rests on eco-logical knowing: 'With joy you will draw water from the wells of salvation' (Isaiah 12:3). Here is a vision of flourishing where water is literally life-giving and a symbol of well-being for this people whom God loves as a precious vineyard, an image which became so important for the evangelists. But God's wise counsel is specifically poured out as ecological counsel:

> Do those who plough for sowing plough continually?
>> Do they continually open and harrow their ground?
> When they have levelled its surface,
>> do they not scatter dill, sow cummin,
> and plant wheat in rows
>> and barley in its proper place,
>> and spelt as the border?
> For they are well-instructed;
>> their God teaches them.
>
> (Isaiah 28:23–6)

This wisdom I link with the sabbatical seventh year, letting the land lie fallow, as well as with the Isaian insistence that God is responsible for the limits of creation:

> Have you not known? Have you not heard?
>> Has it not been told you from the beginning?
>> Have you not understood from the foundations of the
>>> earth? . . .
> To whom then will you compare me,
>> or who is my equal? says the Holy One.
>
> (Isaiah 40:21, 25)

But what could this ecological wisdom mean for sacra-mental and worshipping communities? This is my concern: in this alternative cultural imaginary I develop, new possibilities unfold. Imagination cannot remain at the level of seeing or hearing at an abstract level, but must become embedded, embodied in our ecclesial praxis. This is the challenge for a spirituality of hoping, which, so far, has the ingredients of *attending to time, resisting and dangerously remembering*. If conversion and reconciliation are at the heart of Christian ecclesial identity, these call us, before it is too late, to focus on a reconversion to the earth, a listening to the crying of the earth, as one writer put it.[28] Through our imagined futures, the imperative is to connect the neglect and suffering of the earth with vulnerable people, with women, children and indigenous peoples the world over: with the women who walk ever further to find water, the women who allowed their bodies to be hacked to pieces to save the trees of the forests in India,[29] with the children of Chernobyl who will always carry the scars of the nuclear explosion – if they survive at all.

But it also means putting the flourishing of the whole bioregional community at the heart of our eucharistic *diakonia* or service. Reimagine the image of the feast on the holy mountain (Isaiah 25) as a eucharistic image: bread in a theology of flourishing asks that we consider who labours to grow wheat and whether their wages are just; which farmers are deprived of a livelihood because of genetically manipulated crops. Wine, whereas it does symbolise the joy and abundance of the feast, and in a theology of *salvation* symbolises the giving of innocent blood; yet – with a different focus – in a theology of *flourishing* asks what it means in our communities where addictions to drugs, alcohol, money or even perpetual youth destroy the possibilities of flourishing.

A renewed sacramental imaginary can challenge us to recover the power of liturgy to transform; where praise of creation, interwoven with prophetic lament at what we have lost and what we mourn, giving ourselves time to grieve the death of the forests and the pollution of air and soil, touches the wellsprings of our compassion and unleashes the power to transform, sowing the seeds of outrageous hope for the renewal of creation. And in fact, it is because of this ecological wisdom that the seventh-century Byzantine theologian Maximus the Confessor considered liturgy to be an *ethical science*:

> This whole reality is science because it is the achievement of all knowledge concerning God and divine realities and virtues accessible to men [people]. It is knowledge because it genuinely lays hold of the truth and offers a lasting experience of God.[30]

David Toolan writes that,

> Liturgy is the big clue: here we regularly take fossil fuels, stone, metals, silicon, water, fire, grain, grape, animal stuffs, air-waves and sound – indeed, as much space-time as we can sensuously lay our hands on – and convert it into a gathering of voices, a ceremony of praise and thanksgiving.[31]

Whereas it has been said that, in the context of violence and repression in Chile, Guatemala and Central America, *torture* best expressed the imagination of the state, in contrast, *the Eucharist is the imagination of the prophetic Church*.[32] It is an imagination which itself nurtures a different *praxis of sacrifice*, which inspires a simplicity of lifestyle because of our love for the earth and all her creatures. The Dominican theologian Richard Woods calls this an ascetics, or ascesis, not of mortification but of care, care for the earth and all vulnerable creatures, all vulnerable human bodies who suffer with the earth.[33]

And so, we have come full circle. From the prophet's lament that 'my people go into exile without knowledge' (Isaiah 5:13) to the realisation that the lack of an *imaginary of flourishing* destroyed the connection between the devastation of the earth and the suffering of vulnerable people; to the recovery of ecological wisdom through the transforming power of liturgy, where the themes of destroyed earth and flourishing of new creation become the commitment of a community, first to mourn, but then to reorganise energies for action. The emphasis is on *Leitourgia*, the authentic work of the gathered community: a people who grieve, lament, give thanks, and at the same *work* to free the land from the poison of pesticide, the long death of radiation and nuclear winter, and the injustice of being wrenched away from the ownership of indigenous peoples, with all the conflict and complexity this means.[34] This knowing refuses boundaries between thinking and feeling, between academic science and practical wisdom, in favour of the culturally inherited wisdom of ordinary people, the bodily wisdom we share with other earth creatures.

And, finally, a spirituality of imagination demands urgently that this be embodied and earthed, materialised, and not stuck at a level of abstraction. Liberating imaginations continually seek expression even in the most oppressive and death-like conditions. Like children who drew butterflies in the ghettos of Theresienstadt, when the Nazis occupied the former Czechoslovakia; like the children who drew birds of peace as the bombs fell over Sarajevo, liberated imagination summons through both the table-praxis of Eucharist and life-praxis of reconversion to the earth: *this is the daily nourishment of the outrageous pursuit of hope.*

THE RE-EMERGENCE OF THE SPIRIT: A NEW LANGUAGE OF THE SACRED IN A POSTMODERN WORLD

INTRODUCTION: A CONTEMPORARY DILEMMA: HOW SHOULD THE SPIRIT LEVEL MIRROR OUR AGE?

This chapter continues the thread of the new cultural imagination needed at this time of expectation and openness. The aim is to take further the argument that European culture needs a breakthrough at the level of imagination – which is where a spirituality of hoping points. For a decree has gone out, not from Caesar Augustus, but from the Blair Government, that there shall be a stately Pleasure Dome, not in Xanadu but in Greenwich (apologies to Coleridge![1]) to celebrate the irruption of the third millennium. In these caverns measureless (except in the fortune they cost!) elaborate schemes are being embodied: but none have been wrangled about more than the spirit level and what it should contain. This raises the question whether there is simply a vacuum in the Zeitgeist of our age, or merely a death of creativity and religious zeal. Part of the problem has been the disagreement as to whether the Spirit Level should represent Christianity principally, since this millennium counts back to the birth of

Christ, or acknowledge the truth that Britain is now a multi-faith and multicultural society, where, indeed, an increasing number do not profess a religious faith at all. Or must it be admitted that what would truly represent the Zeitgeist is so far from being inspirational, that – in unconscious modesty, if not shame! – the public mind draws the line at creating more theme parks, Disneylands, or Gardens of Eden for Tele-tubbies?[2]

Forty years ago, Martin Buber called for an hour of silence over the name of God: I wonder if he realised that the silence would last so long. But I wonder, too, if at this juncture, it is only the initiative and grace of this banished God which will call us out of this silence and lead this end-of-the-millennium culture, stammering with a new and unaccustomed humility, into a process of new naming and discovery?

A POSTMODERN DILEMMA

It is beyond dispute that the 'postmodern condition' is part of the current dilemma. Since the (presumed) death of the grand narratives, and the overthrowing of the conviction that Europe (first, historically speaking, and subsequently North America) possessed a superior, universal culture which fuelled European colonising endeavours, and continued to produce a mindset keeping Eurocentric thought dominating much of the world, postmodernism has continued to undermine many of the assumptions and constructions of western culture. There is hardly an aspect of what is grandly called *civilisation* that has not been challenged: for example, the concepts underpinning law, western post-Enlightenment rationality, and even the construction of the human person. Truth is now, so it is said, relative to context, partial, and must surrender its universal pretensions. Attention must be paid to gaps, ruptures in the grand stories, and especially to the silences of the great texts. What they omit becomes as important as what they do say.

Two examples are offered as illustration. Recently, I participated in a conference in the Caribbean island of St Vincent in the Grenadines, on 'God in History in the Caribbean'. For these Caribbean theologians, who saw their past as a history of slavery, whose present is experienced as increasing struggles in a context of multiple sufferings through globalisation, theology began for them in a space of confrontation.[3] They spoke of the *forced nature of theology*, meaning that a Eurocentric theology had been and still is forced upon them, with no attention or analysis from their own context. Hence the need to confront this, to construct an identity, a rootedness, in a contemporary context of new forms of slavery now resulting from the effects of unchecked global capitalism. I heard in this context many expressions of cultural despair, a sense of 'we're going nowhere'. From their vantage point, the question was not the constructed nature of reality, but *who did the constructing, and what space there is for the creation of alternative identities.*

The second example is from the discourse of feminist theology. In its initial honeymoon days in the sixties, the global language of sisterhood was powerful: 'Unless all women are free, no woman is free' ran the adage. But this was soon shown to be yet another manifestation of a globalising universalism, where Euro-American analysis obscured the distinctive oppressions and struggles of communities of women whose major struggle was principally, to quote women of colour in the United States, against racism not sexism, or, to cite specific struggles from Asia and Latin America, militarism and ineluctable, mutually reinforcing spirals of poverty. That very language of relation, connection and mutuality, and a spirituality based on notions of bonding and wholeness, which appeared inspiring up till the end of the eighties, threatened to be drowned in the assertion of difference, diversity, and a plea not to suppress 'the otherness of the other'.[4]

The sharpness of these two examples highlights the difficulty in articulating a theology of the Holy Spirit, the Spirit of God whose identity is expressed in Christian tradition as *vinculum amoris* ('bond of love'), the divine 'glue' uniting and bonding communities across cultures, cultures now apparently pressing towards distinctiveness and diversity.

Many factors here need unpacking, the first set political and the second theological. No one can be unaware that the great need of these times is sensitivity to the identity of subcultures, who protest against their submersion under dominant powers, in some cases after a long history of injustices and systemic oppression. The fall of communism in 1989 has unleashed a surge of nationalism in the Balkan states, as well as in the former Soviet Union. At this moment of writing, European governments are only too aware of the continuing tragedies in Kosovo, the recent anguish of the Kurdish people, the Basque separatists – the list goes on. Each of these examples has a complex and painful history: no one struggle is reducible to the other. But what cries out for attention is the insistence on recognition of the irreducibility of identity, the suffering within which each distinctive group hangs on to this identity, demanding recognition of the injustices they endure, their right to their own voice and place in the sun. Michel Foucault spoke, prophetically, of the 'insurrection of the subjugated knowledges';[5] and this is exactly what Isaiah was calling for in the context of maintaining Jewish identity in Babylon, an identity endangered by being assimilated to Babylonian values and idols. Isaiah, like Foucault, insisted on the Jewish people's distinctiveness in the eyes of God.

But the question here is whether there is a new language of the Spirit for this changed context. Whether, in other words, there is a language of connection which respects difference, and is based on a renewed, more modest universalism, without reproducing the old dominant, hegemonic language, suppressing difference, forcing unity where none could coexist with justice.

First, I ask if there are trajectories of the Spirit within Jewish and Christian traditions functioning as resource in this quest.

TRAJECTORIES OF THE SPIRIT

It is understood that Christians in the West are confessing to a disastrous neglect of the Holy Spirit; that Christians acknowledge that Christocentrism, or overfocus on the Christ figure, has both obscured the third person of the Trinity, but also allowed us to identify Christ with worldly powers. The eternal Logos became synonymous with the imperialism of empire. Christomonism, or what the German liberation theologian Dorothee Sölle even called Christofascism, still rears its ugly head where the Church allies itself with repressive regimes (and it is humbling to reflect on many aspects of the Church's involvement with the current episode with the former President Pinochet of Chile); this emphasis obscures the humiliated face of the crucified Jesus in history, suppresses a role for the Spirit, and seems to encourage the overemphasis on the exaggerated rationalism of the West. Yet, in the last thirty years, we have begun to see a reaction, a reaction which I will argue shows certain ambiguities.

For, to begin with the obvious, in the mushrooming of the charismatic movements the increasing popularity of the Holy Spirit is remarkable. Instead of being, as the late journalist Gerald Priestland described, 'the Guest who came to dinner and stayed on to become a member of the family',[6] the charismatic Spirit is at the centre of all kinds of movements. Imagery of wind and fire has regained a new power; there is a new emphasis on charismatic gifts of prophecy, tongues and healing; and the fruits of the Spirit are manifest in the enthusiasm for prayer, the healing ministry, new roles and ministry for lay people, and an ecumenical commitment.[7]

Second, it must be acknowledged that the Pentecostal churches (where the inspiration of the Spirit is pivotal) as a global phenomenon are the fastest growing groups in all Christianity.[8] There are over 400 million Pentecostal Christians today, a group growing faster than either Christian fundamentalism or militant Islam, and the stress in these and related groups is on *qualitative religious experience.* But it must be stressed that emphasis on experience as a touchstone for religious authenticity is a factor uniting feminist spirituality, liberation theology, charismatic movements and a range of New Age groups. But, as Harvey Cox writes in a recent book, this emphasis has emerged in waves throughout Christian history:

> During the Protestant reformation, Luther and Calvin stressed scripture against tradition. During the Methodist revivals, Wesley and his followers accepted experience over both. During my boyhood, the emphasis in my Baptist denomination was being sharply challenged by fundamentalists who were insisting on doctrinal purity.[9]

But the question, of course, is the theological meaning and interpretation of the phenomena attributed to the Holy Spirit. For example, *glossolalia*, speaking in tongues, claiming scriptural authenticity in Paul's theology of the Spirit, has been described variously as an hysterical outburst, as fostering dependency and infantile behaviour, as a deeply mystical experience (as in Jonathan Edwards' famous account of his wife's seventeen days of mystical experiences) or, as Cox writes,

> a mystical-experiential protest against an existing religious language that has turned stagnant or been corrupted. It

almost always takes place amongst people who are themselves culturally displaced, and often politically or socially
disinherited as well. It is a form of cultural subversion, a
liberating energy that frees people to praise God. Further-
more, it helps to create a new religious sub-culture.[10]

The idea of the politically or socially disinherited people
seems to fit better in post-Sandinista Nicaragua or Chile, than
it does in Holy Trinity, Brompton! Clearly there are personal
needs being met by new revelations of the Spirit in vastly
different historical climates. John Taylor, the former Bishop
of Winchester, wrote as early as 1972:

> They [movements of the spirit] are a passionate expression
> of self-concern. Need is met. Unconscious tensions are
> being released. Loneliness is appeased. Sickness is healed.
> Uncertainties about the future are resolved. Inarticulate
> weakness finds rich self-expression.[11]

But it would be simplistic to analyse movements of the Spirit
one-sidedly as simply meeting personality needs, or as being
restricted to an inner life. Yet one cannot avoid the impression
that many of these movements are a reaction to what is
perceived to be the failure of freedom movements, or of
solutions along political and liberation theological lines;
instead of justice, people prefer to seek for satisfying lives of
a more inward-looking nature, together with a decidedly more
conservative political stance. Yet there is a compulsion to give
this inward, conservative stance a community expression . . .
Consider for a moment Chile as an example, and the link
between worldly prosperity (God blesses in a material way
those who are totally committed to the Spirit) and a conservative theology and anthropology. Yet, at the same time, is the
Spirit not crying out in the name of the silenced voices of
the Disappeared?

Notwithstanding, it is undeniable that many charismatic

movements have recourse to the headship metaphor of Paul and see the husband in full authority over his wife, with privileged access to God, thus legitimising traditional patriarchal theology; they see charity as exercised within the immediate community, and avoid a confrontation with what Walter Wink would call 'the powers', or what Roman Catholic theology calls structural sin.

But this is only one trajectory. Historically, there are many examples of the power of the Spirit acting in a prophetic way, disrupting the status quo, and at the cutting edge of social change and ferment. From the Montanist movements of the second century, where women were prominent in leadership, to the theology of Hildegarde in the twelfth century, to the origins of the Society of Friends, the Quakers, there have been remarkable incidences of the Spirit's power. And not all of these have been marked by ecstatic phenomena, but equally by discernment, silence and waiting on the Spirit. A little-known occurrence of the Spirit's activity was the story of Jemima Wilkinson, a young New England Quaker farm girl, who was converted during the New Light revival of 1774, expelled by the Quakers and then became critically ill. Through her visions, where the angels promise 'Room, room for thee, and for everyone', as Catherine Keller relates:

> Jemima Wilkinson seems to have read her own epiphany through the biblical apocalypse, omitting the violence and the exclusive masculine agency of the original vision:
>
>> And the angels said, The time is at hand, when God will lift up his hand, a second time, to recover the remnant of his People, whose day is not yet over; and the angels said, The Spirit of Life from God had descended to earth, to warn a ... perishing, dying world, to flee from the wrath which is to come; and to give an invitation to the Lost Sheep of the house of Israel to come home; and

was waiting to assume the Body which God had prepared for the Spirit to dwell in.[12]

This extraordinary story relates how the young girl gave up her own body and was taken possession of by the spirit, when she became known as the *Universal Publick Friend*, a transformed, spirit-filled person. No gendered pronouns applied any longer. Apparently, she preached and wandered, celibate though not demanding this of her followers, 'flamboyant on a saddle of blue velvet and white leather, infamous for beautiful loose black curls in a time when women bound and covered their hair' (Keller, p. 235). Finally a Utopian community was founded near Seneca Lake, New York, in which property was held in common, non-violence was the rule, and a 'relative egalitarianism' prevailed. The community's name was 'New Jerusalem'. In passing, let us note the name of this remarkable woman, *'Universal' Publick Friend*: does this give a clue that the Spirit can introduce a new universalism which could shatter the old relations of dominance and suppression of the identities of cultural minorities?

At this point I introduce the most ancient trajectory of all, the Spirit as breath of life.

SPIRIT, BREATH OF LIFE

This, the most ancient witness to the Spirit, from the biblical sources, is often, if not overlooked, at any rate interpreted in a narrow way. Whether Genesis 1:1 is at any rate translated as 'A wind from God swept over the face of the waters' (NSRV, NEB), or 'God's spirit hovered over the water' (JB),[13] the creative power of the Spirit at the dawn of creation, breathing life into all creatures, is a fundamental trajectory of the Spirit faith traditions. Here is the intuition of the energy of connection (which has been fundamental to my own theology).[14]

Second, the breath of life emerges from the formless void, the chaos, the *tohu bohu*. Here it is crucial to avoid the easy slide into assuming that the spirit = order over against chaos, unity as opposed to distinctive identity.[15] The more reflection on western history there is, the more the postmodern Christian is drawn to admit the pitfalls of identity based on enforced assimilation: for example, European identity is assumed to be Christian, yet there have been groups of Jews and Muslims in Europe for hundreds of years. Again, the foundations of Christianity (or Christendom) are assumed to be essentially European, a 'fact' ignoring the contributions of North Africa and Asia. Many innocent people have been condemned to death – notably women during the great European witch hunt – for factors based on a mixture of fear of the unknown and of difference, gender discrimination, elimination of otherness and self-interest, rather than any criminal offence. To assume that the Spirit must lead to homogeneity and is the glue binding like with like risks rendering such oppression invisible. It is a far cry from valuing the element of wildness ('The Wild Bird who Heals', as one writer puts it[16]), the unpredictability, and hiddenness of the Spirit who leads into the unknown and can overturn human categories and boundaries.[17]

Third, the intuition of the Spirit as energy of connection acquires a new dimension by the intermeshing of God's Spirit and the human spirit. Consider the words of Psalm 51:10–12:

> Create in me a clean heart, O God,
>> and put a new and right spirit within me.
> Do not cast me away from your presence,
>> and do not take away your holy spirit from me.
> Restore to me the joy of your salvation,
>> and sustain in me a willing spirit.

And later:

> The sacrifice acceptable to God is a broken spirit;
>> a broken contrite heart, O God,
>>> you will not despise.

(Psalm 51:17)

It is not only that God's Spirit and the human spirit have a mutual dependency, but that the human spirit, and the life-breath of all living things, flow from the creative Divine Spirit. It is this intermeshing dynamism which is so striking in this renewed theology of the Spirit – both a recovery of an ancient dynamism but, in the present context, emphasising God's Spirit-human spirit within a myriad interconnections with the earth. Here is how Elizabeth Johnson sums up Hildegarde of Bingen's theology of spirit:

> The Spirit is life, movement, colour, radiance, restorative stillness in the din. She pours the juice of contrition into hardened hearts. Her power makes dry twigs and withered souls green again with the juice of life. She purifies, absolves, strengthens, heals, gathers the perplexed, seeks the lost. She plays the music in the soul, being herself the melody of praise and joy. She awakens mighty hope, blowing everywhere the winds of renewal in creation.[18]

John Taylor, in his inspirational book, *The Go-Between God*, envisioned this energy of the Spirit as the mutual life-force between people, using the Annunciation as an inspirational motif.[19] The energy radiating between the Holy Spirit and Mary is the connecting energy at the heart of incarnation. This epiphany is experienced over and over again, where the Spirit acts as go-between: he cites Edwin Muir – but there are a range of resources in this inspirational work:

> See, they have come together, see,
> While the destroying minutes flow,
> Each reflects the other's face

Till heaven in hers and earth in his
Shine steady there . . .

But through the endless afternoon
These neither speak nor movement make,
But stare into their deepening trance
As if their gaze would never break.[20]

A similar intuition is behind feminist theology's development of relational theology, inspired, among other sources, by
Martin Buber's insight as to the *Thou-ness* at existence's core:
'In the beginning is the relation, and in the relation is the
power which creates the world, through us and with us and
by us, you and I, you and we, and none of us alone.'[21]

But this insight of the *thou* at reality's core can now be
further developed in an ecological and ecofeminist way, which
I would argue is even closer to the biblical sources. The
point of doing this is to avoid the perilous slippage back
into spiritualising and disembodying of the Spirit. This, the
perennial temptation of western theology, undermines all
the solid embodying, materialising, earthing efforts of current
spirituality. In her ecological theology, Sallie McFague views
the universe organically through the metaphor of God's body,
'a body enlivened and empowered by the divine spirit'.[22] She
builds on the symbolism of the Spirit as wind, breath, as the
energy knitting together the lives of planets, animals and all
living creatures; breath is even more fundamental than food
and water, since we actually exist from breath to breath. Yet
Spirit is more: spirit is courage, grit, determination, *vitality* –
a term now used by Moltmann in his theology of creation –
the dynamism sweeping through a group, a movement, and
even permeating a place.

McFague prefers spirit as a metaphor over heart, body, or
soul, first, because it 'undercuts anthropocentrism and pro-
motes cosmocentrism' (p. 144). Second, because it suggests
that 'God is not primarily the orderer and controller of the

universe but its source and empowerment, the breath that enlivens and energises it' (p. 145), the breath that is its vitality and dynamism:

> Thus, in a spirit theology, we might see ourselves as united with all other living creatures through the breath that moves through all parts of the body, rather than as the demilords who order and control the universe. (p. 145)

Aesthetically, ethically and ecologically this has appeal. This is far from a homogenising and assimilating spirit: more an energy inviting the respect for diversity. It is also claimed to relate well to postmodern science, stressing both autonomous and integrative or relational elements of every organism. The physicist Paul Davies describes the theory of super-symmetry whereby the basic units of the universe are not particles but 'wiggling motions of strings, like notes on a piano wire'.[23] If, at the most basic level, the movement of creation is a double dynamism, towards relation and towards personal survival (both personal integrity and relational growth), is this not more helpful than the postmodern insistence on rupture and the constructed nature of reality? Theologically, the stress on God's continual presence, not intervention, God's empowerment, God's presence as direction-giving (in process theology, 'God's lure'), is the strength of this metaphor.

Further, in an age threatened with ecological extinction, any theological response emerges in a context where the narratives of modernity practising lying on a grand scale are still exerting their power: I think of a text like Heidegger's 'The Question concerning Technology', which in the wake of the atrocities of Auschwitz, and his own collaboration with Nazi ideology, could still, in 1953, refer to 'man' as not yet having reaching the brink of facing what he called the 'Standing reserve',[24] in spite of the fact that, after the *Shoah* ('Catastrophe'), the 'Final Solution', there was no doubt at all that a brink had been reached and a chasm had been crossed.

The Outrageous Pursuit of Hope

There are many examples of truth-denying narratives. As I write, the horrors of Serbian ethnic cleansing emerge, accompanied by denials and confusions, in a war where evasion of the truth on both sides is observed. It is generally admitted that in the wake of the death of communism it was very difficult to discern the truth, even to know what it was to tell a lie. As the last chapter indicated, we live at the moment amidst a massive denial of the extent of the ecological crisis. These truth-denying narratives seem to have produced a psychic numbness, a massive denial of the problems threatening the earth. There has to be another way forward for a theology of hope.

So I revisit Isaiah's call upon the Spirit made at a time when any semblance of a grand narrative had lost credibility for the children of Israel. But I do this, putting alongside it the contradictions that confront western culture: on the one hand, the arrogance of seeking an even wider viewpoint on society – the view from outer space. At the very time of trying to leave Descartes's narrow rationalised heritage behind, the cold, objective view of the world of the detached observer, arrogant humanity seems to be demanding a wider and wider view, whether from a space capsule or Foucault's *panopticon*. And yet, on the other hand, the humble embodiedness of the Spirit is showing itself in contrasting ways. Shrines spring up at the places connected with accidents;[25] people of the peace movements release flocks of doves into the air; the sacredness of ordinary life is rediscovered.[26] Young people set off on journeys – to Iona, to Taizé, Lindisfarne, Bardsey Island – inviting the possibility of change and transformation. Is this energy, bringing together disparate people in new understandings, the beginning of a spirituality of hope for the twenty-first century?

I suggest that the ecological model of the Spirit, evoking multiple biotic interdependencies, should be a model for other levels of liberating mutuality. For God and nature have always been intertwined – it is philosophies of separation and superiority that have blocked a deeper truth. Mark Wallace argues that a biotic reconciliation takes place when we practise unity, intimacy and reciprocity with both humans and non-human creatures.[27] This unity, which is spirit-promoted, erases artificial boundaries and generates an ethic of transgression, a liberating courage to reject all that prevents flourishing, thus enabling a boundless openness to life.

The Spirit can be re-encountered as the creator of multiple levels of mutuality, in full respect for difference and diversity. The Spirit as *vinculum amoris* (bond of love), *vinculum caritatis* (bond of charity), can be experienced as crossing the false boundaries between human and non-human (and of course the boundaries of sexual and racial difference). Wallace writes that just as the Spirit is the bond of love within the Trinity, and 'the inner minister of the human heart who instructs and sanctifies the faithful to seek the welfare of the other', she is also 'the power of dynamic union within creation who continually animates, integrates, and preserves all life in the cosmos'.[28]

If it is threatening for humanity to face the fact that we are formed of the soil and mud, perhaps this is a salutary corrective to 'reaching for the moon'. Not only that, but the Spirit faces us with the challenge that stewardship of the earth is an inadequate model when all life forms have inherent value:

> The Spirit is the green face of God, the intercessory force for peace and solidarity in a world saturated with sacrificial violence, the power of renewal within creation as the creation groans in travail and waits with eager longing for environmental justice . . .[29]

I wonder if the clue is exactly where we stand now in history: that at this *fin-de-siècle* moment, the silence, the waiting, the hoping of those who keep faith, those, that is, on the margins of this culture of contentment, indicate the birth of something new. If the Spirit is associated with bringing to birth ('Fill the earth, bring it to birth', as the old hymn put it), then the imagery of the cosmic egg is timely. The Spirit is watchful for the moment where the cracks in the discourses of violence appear, where humanity at last admits vulnerability in having no answers, and commits itself at last *to a different kind of listening*.

In this culture of narcissism, by definition self-enclosed, effective initiative in cracking open the false truths on which we have built our houses cannot come from humanity alone. But this is not to fall back into traditional interventionist language about God: it is to believe in the power of healing connections as the Spirit's work of grace. Scripture insists that only the sin against the Holy Spirit is unforgivable.[30] Does this mean that, in so far as we are a culture setting ourselves completely against life-giving vitality and crying 'Evil, be thou my good', as Satan did in *Paradise Lost*[31] – at this moment we block ourselves from the Spirit? Thus would we and all living things choose to rob ourselves of any future. But, even then, God's freedom could begin again in the smouldering ashes of this civilisation. Weep for the city, cried Jesus, but instead we are deaf and hardened of heart – to use Isaiah's metaphors – as the city burns.

Yet, in the midst of institutionalised deafness, one powerful way in which hope and courage are kept alive, one way in which the Spirit finds cracks in the culture, is through the presence of those suffering for justice, the community of witnesses, living and dead, the 'subaltern presence' (to use an almost outrageous pun) of Revelation 6:9:

The Re-Emergence of the Spirit

When he broke the fifth seal I saw under the altar the souls of those who had been slaughtered for God's word and the testimony they bore. They gave a great cry: 'How long, sovereign Lord, holy and true, must it be before thou wilt vindicate us and avenge our blood on the inhabitants of the earth?' (Revelation 6:9–10 NEB)

To remember and celebrate the presence and the witness of the community of saints, from *all* faiths all over the world, suffering and being murdered because they stand for truth and justice: this awakens a new awareness of the transgressive Spirit kindling the fires of resistance and creating a new source of mutuality across and beyond boundaries.

It was by keeping alive the dangerous memory of the Jewish people that Isaiah rekindled faith in the Spirit's prophetic power. 'Remember your own calling to be the light of the nations' is a revitalising call. But there is also a unique role for the person referred to as the Servant of the Lord in rekindling a nation's hope.

Many arguments rage as to the identity of this figure, who appears as a distinct figure in four passages of the text. Was it the prophet himself? His son? Ahaz? Cyrus, the Persian emperor? Was it Israel's own identity as servant? Or was it the faithful remnant of Israel, the true and righteous Israel? The *sensus plenior* of Christian tradition of course ascribes the full identity of the servant to Jesus. The richness of the Good Friday Liturgy builds on this text, as well as the beauteous solemnity of Handel's *Messiah*. 'He was despised and rejected . . .' The discussion rumbles on as to whether Jesus understood his own suffering in terms of this text.[32] The weight of scholarship seems to agree that this identification was much later than the life of Jesus himself and that even the idea of vicarious suffering developed gradually.[33]

My concern here is to explore what insight Isaiah offers about the Spirit through the struggles of the Servant, in the context of the transgressive role of the Spirit I am developing. First of all, the sheer shock value of the context of these passages, in that God is using Cyrus, the Persian leader, as the instrument of grace to lead Israel back to freedom, certainly shatters a few categories. Why should redemption come from a non-Jewish source?

> Though you do not know me, I arm you
> that men may know from the rising to the setting of the
> sun
> that, apart from me, all is nothing.
>
> (Isaiah 45:5b–6a JB)

Leaving aside the militaristic imagery of this passage, the insight is unmistakable, that God is to be known far beyond the confines of Israel. But the Spirit-filled Servant who will bring true justice to the nations,

> . . . does not break the crushed reed,
> nor quench the wavering flame.
>
> (Isaiah 42:3 JB)

This is a passage cited later by Matthew with reference to Jesus. In other words, the Spirit is present to the vulnerable, the marginalised and those on the edges of despair. The spirit-filled Servant is empowered not only to minister to Israel but to be

> 'the light of the nations
> so that my salvation will reach the ends of the earth'.
>
> (Isaiah 49:6 JB)

There is no room here for restricting movements of redeeming grace to privileged contexts. It seems that a modest universalism is encouraged – but inspired by the humility of the servant, not the power of the conquistador.

Is it this humility which Jesus advocates, in the only reference he makes to his own heart (Matthew 11:28–30), inspired by the Isaian Servant Song: 'Learn from me; for I am gentle and humble in heart'? Not a pious meekness, but a language of inexhaustible compassion, a humility recognising that there are no quick-fix solutions, in a brutal, broken-hearted world; but a recognition that the context for the Servant, as for millions today, is suffering, suffering from which there is no foreseeable happy outcome. In the midst of this anguish, the Servant pursues hope, outrageously, hope grounded in God the vindicator. In the real court of law, there is no prosecution, no case against the Servant, because though crushed and disfigured with suffering, yet in heart and spirit the Servant is hungering for righteousness.

Many interpretations of this, the most famous of the Servant Songs, have produced distorted eulogies for vicarious suffering, resulting in a blindness to oppression, excusing the suffering of the innocent, because ultimately the Servant's suffering is vindicated. Notably, domestic violence endured by women has been tolerated, excused, with a veil drawn over it, as women have been encouraged to endure in the name of marital peace. But it does not behove us in the West to excuse or explain away the sufferings of anyone, especially any oppressed group in society. Just as the sufferings of slaves in the nineteenth century could not be justified by appeal to the supposed redemptive value of suffering, nor can racist violence today, abuse of women and children, or the newer slavery in the form of crippling debts in the Two-Thirds world be given any similar justification.

But, having said that, is there no meaning for suffering and sacrifice? In a theology of prophetic hoping, surely it is the persons, groups and communities living out lives of commit-ment to right and just relation, hungering for righteousness, who transform the notion of servanthood? Who are prepared to suffer the blows, the loss of status, to keep the language of integrity alive?

It may be that the language of servanthood no longer

expresses the role of the Spirit as breath of life and healing. There is one text in the New Testament that admonishes us not to 'grieve the Holy Spirit of God' (Ephesians 4:30). So the Spirit grieves with the wounds of people and earth. But is this grief the beginning of *healing relationality*? Is this what 'and by his bruises we are healed' (Isaiah 53:5b), the most profound words of all in Isaiah's fourth Servant Song, are pointing to? That is, the Servant's afflictions are shared by the voluntary dedication of prophetic people and communities: so, the hungering after justice of the righteous, the under-the altar presence of those with us yearning for justice – in Pinochet's Chile, as well as in the deserts where the women wait for rains, in Mandela's Soweto, where a language other than violence is at last being painfully forged, in the silent voices of those condemned to a life in psychiatric institutions, the children at the gate, who, as the poet wrote, 'will not go away and cannot pray'[34] – these are the fellow pilgrims with the Servant in the outrageous pursuit of hope. The Spirit creates this language, far beyond words, in the fragile bonding, the vulnerable strands of connection (think of the lonely imprisonment of Aung San Suu Kyi in Burma), the forms of solidarity which are effective (think of the Jubilee 2000 campaign) across different contexts, kneading hope, where none seems rationally possible, because, as Isaiah's voice so poetically speaks:

Then shall your light break forth like the dawn
and soon you will grow healthy like a wound newly
    healed . . .
You will be like a well-watered garden,
like a spring whose waters never fail.

(Isaiah 58:8a, 11b NEB)

Wherever the flickering sparks are fanned to flame, wherever candles are lit in the darkness, the Spirit-filled servants of God, be they individuals or communities, be they the creatures of the wounded earth itself, reveal that even in the deepest affliction hope is not extinguished:

> I believe that behind the mist the sun waits.
> I believe that beyond the dark night it is raining stars . . .
> They will not rob me of hope, it shall not be broken . . .
> It shall not be broken.[35]

Hyun Kyung's sermon in Canberra (Assembly of the World Council of Churches, 1991) illustrates many of these points. First, she invoked the Holy Spirit in terms of the Spirit of the oppressed, from the murdered spirits of the Amazon rainforest, to the spirits of exploited women, and indigenous peoples, victims of the Holocaust and Hiroshima, and all other life forms that, like the Liberator, 'our brother Jesus', have been tortured and killed. A truly powerful subaltern presence!

But her closing words for me sum up the challenge of this chapter: how to understand the presence of the Spirit as a new language of the sacred, being faithful to the limits of history and context and yet to the language of creativity and connection that admits of no narrow restrictions:

> Dear sisters and brothers, with the energy of the Spirit let us tear apart all walls of division and the culture of death which separates us. And let us participate in the Holy Spirit's economy of life, fighting for our life on this earth, in solidarity with all living beings . . . Wild wind of the holy Spirit blow to us. Let us welcome her, letting ourselves go in her wild rhythm of life. Come Holy Spirit, renew the whole of creation. Amen.[36]

'WISDOM'S FEAST': THE CELEBRATION OF COSMIC INTEGRITY

INTRODUCTION

How, then, at the end of this exploration, as pilgrims of hoping, is hope to be reawakened and nourished, at the brink of the third millennium? Not merely the hope of the privileged, but the hope of all who are forced to dwell in hopelessness, on the brink of despair?

This book has been exploring a theology of hope through the redeeming of time, subversive strategies for crying freedom, within the context of a spirituality of attentive waiting, dangerously remembering, reimagining what is possible, and resisting. 'Resistance is the secret of joy' is the high point of such a spirituality. Following Isaiah's trajectory of ecological wisdom I have suggested that hope is nurtured within a theology of flourishing, through stimulating a counter-cultural imagination, and through the initiative of the Holy Spirit in cracking open culture, creating new transgressive energies for life, for connection across boundaries. But this, the work of the third millennium, is just beginning. As the poet Denise Levertov wrote:

How could we tire of hope?
so much is in bud.

How can desire fail?
– we have only just begun

to imagine justice and mercy,
only begun to envision

how it might be
to live as siblings with beast and flower,
not as oppressors . . .

So much is unfolding that must complete its gesture,
so much is in bud.[1]

To celebrate all that is in bud is the hope. But where is the place, the graced space to celebrate this, even amidst the tragedies threatening to engulf so many people? I take heart from the conviction of the Latin American biblical theologian Elsa Tamez, that even amidst the apparent collapse of dreams there are good grounds for celebrating.[2] She takes as inspiration that unlikely text, Ecclesiastes: in the midst of the vanity of vanities, she

> finds defiance and hope in the midst of the oppression and hopelessness, in the very simple, present and simple joys of life . . . such as eating, drinking, and enjoying life with one's loved ones, trusting in God who will act with justice in her own good time.

This suggests that there a counter-cultural thrust in true celebration. Elsa Tamez's hope is limited, not utopian in character. Celebrating the small gains, in the ruins of the failure of the grand dreams – as with most of the millenarian revolutions throughout history, this must be the seedbed for a realistic hoping.

To nourish this hoping, the place of grace is, of course, all the communities across the whole spectrum of the spaces where we dwell and work, be they political, or faith-inspired, cultural and aesthetic, earth-loving, those we deliberately choose and those thrust upon us – or perhaps a mixture of many of these strands.

Second, giving content and character to these communities, the creative and transgressive Spirit (explored in the last chapter) is reawakening and revitalising *wisdom communities*. This, I argue, is the context and direction of the work of the Spirit today – the fashioning, the artistry, the creative shape of Wisdom. For the iconography of the figure of Wisdom is part of the new cultural imaginary I have been trying to develop. This *is* one of the links between contemporary searching and the imagined future for the Isaian community. The image of 'Wisdom's Feast' I take from Isaiah 55, but I move beyond Isaiah to other wisdom texts, without losing the prophet's insistence that hope be embodied in history, in a specific context, to flourish within our wisdom communities. First, I ask, what are the roots of this figure of Wisdom, the biblical Sophia (see Illus. 4), in Hebrew *hokmah*?

WHO IS SOPHIA?

> Once upon a time there was Wisdom. There was Wisdom, and she was present everywhere with all the intensity and all the desire of all there was. And once the Word was spoken she and she alone dived into the spaces between the words, blessing the silence out of which new worlds are born. Now, as it was in the beginning, Wisdom is hearing all creation into speech.[3]

These words of the theologian Lucy Tatman express something of the inspirational quality of the figure of Wisdom. Wisdom speaks to an experience deeper than words, touches the imagination and has a mythological significance throughout many civilisations. The wisdom figure referred to is, of course, the biblical wisdom figure of *Hokmah*, or *Sophia* in Greek, imaged as female – hence the reams of literature on Sophia as the feminine or female face of God. The interesting point for my theme is precisely that Sophia enters late into the Bible – she does not appear in the five books of Moses. One suggestion is that she enters at a moment when the prophets (in my case, specifically Isaiah), for reasons I have argued earlier, were inviting the Jewish people to understand the mercy and *shalom* of God in a less exclusive way, beyond the confines of their own nation. I have suggested that this is the linking point with the contemporary world where the Spirit leads us to cross and recross boundaries in order to recognise God's action in new and surprising ways. Spirit–Sophia are united in this role. Hence the constant imagery of Sophia setting a table, summoning people to the feast from the highways and byways. The sheer power of the imagery of the biblical Sophia grips the imagination, as well as evoking the question as to why she could have been forgotten or marginalised by the dominant tradition. Here I map out the strands of activity of Sophia in the Bible and in certain strands of contemporary spirituality.[4]

Like the Spirit, she is creative energy with God at the dawn of creation (Proverbs 8, Ecclesiasticus 24:3–5). She is Teacher (Proverbs 8:1–11). Sometimes she is *both Teacher and what is taught* (Proverbs 4:5–8). To fall in love with Sophia is to fall in love with Wisdom itself. And she can be lover, mother and Teacher all at the same time (Ecclesiasticus 4:11–16). Yet, too, she has an organic link with creation, imaged as *tree and plant* (Ecclesiasticus 24:12–19).[5]

Alongside the scriptural strand is an even older mythological strand. For Sophia is associated with goddess figures from ancient Near Eastern cultures and cosmologies. She is linked with Isis of Egypt, Astarte of Babylon, Asherah of Canaan – whose invisible presence haunts the background of the biblical imagery. We can also associate her with the wisdom goddesses of Greece and Rome (Athene and Minerva), with the mother goddesses of Celtic history, and even with Mother Durga and Lakshmi of Hinduism. So it is not only with the goddess as mother that she is associated, but with the goddess as *wisdom*, and as *embodiment of law*. In Christianity there is a long tradition associating Mary, mother of Jesus, as the daughter of wisdom, imaged as *sedes sapientiae*, 'seat of wisdom'.

Third, developing this, Sophia functions today beyond the Christian community as an empowering figure in women's spiritual journey in many contexts. Thus the theologian Carol Christ depicts her own spiritual journey as one from the darkness of no identity, from nothingness, of being *no-thing*, nothing, in traditional Christian spirituality, to discovering the goddess as a powerful and empowering figure of the divine female, to actually rediscovering and experiencing the figure of the Greek goddess Aphrodite. This led to her giving up her professorship in the United States and living in Greece, where she leads regular pilgrimages in search of the goddess.[6] This particular strand swivels between understanding the goddess as female principle of the divine – supplying the lack in an otherwise totally male cluster of symbols across all religions – and actually recovering the following of some of the ancient goddesses, asking what is their power for the contemporary world.

Since these last two strands depict the rediscovery of Sophia far beyond Christianity and Judaism, it becomes easy to see why, when we add the inspiration of Sophia to specifically Christian feminist liturgies, this has provoked such a negative reaction.[7] Both in Europe and the United States the figure of Sophia-Wisdom – in prayer, art and hymn – has arisen, it would seem spontaneously. I recall that when I was asked to give one of the keynote speeches on women's development at the European Women's Synod in 1996, completely unaware of the powerful role that this symbol would play in the Synod as a whole, I had titled the speech 'Empowered to Lead: Sophia's Daughters Blaze a Trail'.[8] Here, because of the positive reaction of the Muslim women present, for the first time I became aware of the way the symbol of Sophia-Spirit was able to draw disparate communities into empathy and relation.

But because I also have sympathy with the fear of paganism, which always lurks in the background of these discussions, and the reluctance of many Christians to move away from traditional, exclusive male imagery of God, I weave two more strands into the web. For Sophia is also present, powerfully, in Russian Orthodox theology, especially in the work of Pavel Florensky, Vladimir Soloviev and Sergei Bulgakov.[9] For Soloviev, the vision of Sophia as a young girl was inspirational for his whole theological development. Wisdom is 'everything gathered up into one; she is God's go-between in creation'.[10] For Bulgakov, Sophia, or Sophiology, is a way of interpreting all theology, not just a theology of creation: 'Sophiology is a theology of crisis, not of distinction, but of salvation.'[11] In his small book, *The Wisdom of God: A Brief Summary of Sophiology*, he too sees Sophia as feminine.[12] Sophia is at the heart of the Trinity, in that she is what makes the Three share the same nature: Sophia is what makes them *consubstantial*.

But it is her role in culture which I take as crucial for my argument: as Bulgakov writes:

> In contemplating culture which has succumbed to secularisation and paganism, which has lost its inspiration and has no answer to give to the tragedy of history, which seems in fact to have lost all meaning – we realise we can find a spring of living water only by a renewal of our faith in the Sophianic, or theandric meaning of the historical process. As the dome of St Sophia in Constantinople with prophetic symbolism portrays heaven bending to earth, so the Wisdom of God itself is spread like a canopy over our sinful though hallowed world.[13]

It was precisely this sense of Sophia as crisis, judgement, discernment, which I was invoking in my book *The Wisdom of Fools?*[14] Here the figure of Sophia invokes a myth of connected living, non-dualist, ecological, justice-centred and relational life. I opposed this to the *logos* myth, which encapsulated much of the current ethos as competitive, materialistic, success-oriented and individualistic. The idea of Sophia as a metaphor for culture-critique is invoked by Celia Deane-Drummond who has proposed Sophia as a metaphor both for ecological theology and for the development of biotech-nology.[15]

This same Sophianic strand of theology also fascinated the late Thomas Merton, who wrote a prose-poem *Hagia Sophia*, about God entering creation as the feminine figure of Sophia/Wisdom, and seeing the incarnation of Sophia in such figures as Lara in Pasternak's novel, *Doctor Zhivago*.[16]

The final strand builds on these ancient roots – biblical and patristic – of Sophia, namely the steadily insistent way that feminist theology has been working on the integrating of Sophia as a founding doctrinal notion – for example, Elisabeth Schüssler Fiorenza's Wisdom Christology, in her book *Jesus, Miriam's Child, Sophia's Prophet*.[17] Building on this imagery, Elizabeth Johnson has developed Sophia as integral to her trinitarian theology, in her book *She Who Is*.[18] This rich weave of six strands suggest that the figure of Sophia-Wisdom as well as the Spirit has been ignored by western theology to its great impoverishment: the recovery of both is an enrichment both for theology and the impact of theology on society.

How does the Spirit awaken and nourish Sophia-Wisdom communities today? I first look at the wisdom as embodied in the Isaiah communities and then at Christ's own praxis of wisdom especially where this is interwoven with the same inspiration.

Hope for Isaiah becomes embodied and historicised in the
communal praxis of wisdom. It is the lack of wisdom in
the first place that brought ruin to the people. This lack of
wisdom is expressed by the hardening of the heart, the failure
to listen, the pursuit of false gods, and by desires and longings
for the wrong things: the pain of God is poignantly expressed
here:

> I was ready to be sought out by those who did not ask,
>   to be found by those who did not seek me.
> I said. 'Here I am, here I am',
>   to a nation that did not call on my name.
>
> (Isaiah 65:1)

This is the link between the contemporary cultural wilderness
and the exiled children of Israel – a failure of wisdom, because
our desires are set on an ever-receding horizon of wealth, our
happiness measured out in consumerist terms. Is this why the
poet cried, 'Wait without hope, for hope would be hope for
the wrong thing'?[19]

But, in contrast, Isaiah gave content to God's hope, the
yearning of God for the flourishing of people and earth
creatures now, in a vision of messianic peace, not in some
disembodied future, some extravagant Utopia, or in a space
where planet Earth is expendable. Eschatological hope *is* God's
hope embodied and celebrated in the present. The Sophia-
wisdom which Isaiah tried to embody, as we have seen, was
within communities grounding wisdom ecologically. Not
only on the level of communitarian ethics is this to be
embodied but also on the level of the weaving of both inner
and outer dimensions of wisdom: from the deep interiority –
the wellsprings of living water or, in Isaian terms, 'the wells

of salvation' – flow energies fuelling the communal praxis of wisdom.

And this is fundamentally what is meant by embodied wisdom. As Susan Griffin wrote, so movingly, of the way our knowing is connected and rooted in earth knowing:

> Because we know ourselves to be made from this earth. See this grass. The patches of silver and brown. Worn by the wind. The grass reflecting all that lives in the soil. The light. The grass needing the soil. With roots deep in the earth. And patches of silver. Like the patches of silver in our hair. Worn by time . . . because we know ourselves to be made from this earth, because we know the sunlight moves through us, water moves through us, everything moves, everything changes, and the daughters are returned to the mothers. She always comes back. Back from the darkness. And the earth grows green again. So we were moved to feel these things.[20]

Through this earth-knowing we discover the process of gracing space, and place. As the same writer so evocatively describes it:

> And if we find this grace through our labour, with our fingers finding the loose thread in the garment, our ears late at night hearing the cries no one else hears, catching the milk in the pot as it begins to boil, the body bent over rocking, rocking, the pieces of cloth sewn together in patterns, the taste of thyme with rosemary and the different odour of oregano, or the grace, the grace of crisis, the fever . . . the grace of economy, the soup of leftovers . . . the slow opening, the listening, the small possibility, barely audible, nodding, almost inarticulate, yet allowing articulation, words, healing, the eyes acknowledge, the grace of the unspoken, spoken in movement, the hand reaches, the blanket is wrapped around, the arms hold this daily mulish

grace, without which we do not choose to continue, and if we find this, we have something of our own. This is our secret grace, unnamed, invisible, surviving.[21]

This deep, connected knowing was already expressed earlier in a poem by Symeon the New Theologian (949–1022), at the turn from the first to the second millennium. Here, the writer Joanna Macy has substituted for 'Christ' and 'Body' the words 'earth' and 'planet'. (I cite only a small part.)

For if we genuinely love her
we wake up inside Earth's body

where all our body, all over,
every most hidden part of it,
is realised in joy as her,
and she makes us utterly real . . .

and recognised as whole, as lovely,
and radiant in her light,
we awaken as the beloved
in every last part of our body.[22]

Second, Sophia wisdom is practical wisdom – called by Aristotle *phronesis*. (This is why I link Spirit with Sophia: the Spirit is the power of creative energy, transgressive power, prophetic dreaming: *Sophia* shapes this wild dreaming into what is possible for communities to embody.) Practical wisdom addresses the structural causes of the collective folly and misdirected desire. Thus there are now many groups demystifying the economics of capitalism, exploring alternative lifestyles, practising the ethics of resistance. The eco-warriors who dwell in treetops, even if not successful in preventing road development or new runways on airports, at least slow things down and make society contemplate alternatives. The vigils and sit-ins outside peace camps, or acts of defiance outside the Ministry of Defence (always on Ash

Wednesday) have not succeeded in stopping the arms trade to Third World countries: but they embody an ethics of resistance. They compel us at least to think that there is another way. Consumer co-operatives, alternative currencies (LETS), Fair Trade products in the supermarkets, have not toppled the system, but they engage communities of shoppers (yes, that is what we British are – no longer shopkeepers!) in becoming aware that there are alternatives. I recall that once I asked a certain supermarket near my home why they didn't stock Fair Trade Coffee. The manageress asked why I wanted it. When I told her that it meant that the people who grew the coffee would get a fair wage and be able to survive poverty, she replied 'Oh, what a good idea!'

A hunger for practical wisdom is the embodied texture of our hoping. The fact that so many people are now forming coalitions challenging unregulated global capitalism concretises the energies of hope. For example, the *Kairos Europa* document, following the tradition of the South African *Kairos* document, and the Central American *Kairos*, calls on the churches of Europe and on all people with a concern for justice, to build coalitions, communities embodying just alternatives to the systems benefiting only the rich:

> We call upon the churches not to avoid conflict with power and money. Reconciliation can only be real and can only grow on the basis of truth and justice, if the real conflicts of interests are tackled and not avoided. In particular, it cannot grow where lies, semi-truths and repression are commonplace.
>
> 4. *The fundamental decision today of prophetic theology: life for all instead of money for a few.*[23]

But Sophia-prophetic Wisdom is expressed not only as the praxis of just alternatives, the rebuilding of the ruined cities or tackling the structural roots of poverty, from which, according to Isaiah, whole communities become 'like a watered garden',

> like a spring of water
> whose roots never fail.

(Isaiah 58:11)

It is rooted in deep spiritual wisdom, where *both* prophecy and mysticism are at home. Root, branch and spirit are the three dimensions of the Jesse Tree, that great Isaian image which inspired the medieval imagination,[24] which saw its fullness manifested by Jesus, child of Sophia-Wisdom, son of Mary, daughter of Wisdom.

When exploring the revelation of Sophia in Jesus, it is important to remember that Jesus is not the only embodiment of Sophia.[25] Sophia, it has been noted, appears in Scripture at a moment when the prophets were revealing the mercy of God and mission of Israel as *lumen gentium*, light for the nations, beyond the narrow confines of one country.[26]

Jesus begins his ministry by placing himself in the same context as Isaiah: when entering the synagogue and reading the text of Isaiah, 'The Spirit of the Lord is upon me' (Luke 4:18–30), he not only proclaims that this text is fulfilled in his own person, but sets an agenda – the same we are now calling the Jubilee agenda, for contemporary Christic communities of prophetic wisdom.

Sophia is embodied by Jesus, first, in that he listens and learns from poor and uneducated people. But what is the wisdom of poor people? Is this not in danger of being glamorised? Here, as illustration, is one of the stories told by the late Paolo Freire, the Brazilian educationalist': when giving a talk among poor people of Chile, it came to the question time and he faced a dead silence. He, the great educationalist, who believed in empowering the poor, had reduced them to silence by the sheer weight of his own learning. So he challenged them to a game. He would first ask a question, and then they would ask him one. They would write the scores on a board: if one side did not know the answer the other side would score:

> First question: 'What is the Socratic maieutic?'
> General guffawing. Score one for me.
> 'Now it's your turn to ask me a question,' I said.
> There was some whispering, and one of them tossed out
> a question:
> 'What's a contour curve?'
> I couldn't answer. I marked down one to one.
> 'What importance does Hegel have in Marx's thought?'
> Two to one.
> 'What's soil-liming?'
> Two to two.[27]

And so it went on until the score was ten/ten. By this game the peasants began to realise that they did know — lots of things. But they were not convinced that their knowledge would count as real, valued knowledge in the academy — and they would be right. Sophia as practical knowledge, *phronesis*, is not esteemed as intellectual learning — in fact is ranked fairly low in current rationalist hierarchies of knowledge.

The Wells for India team has seen this very impasse in our involvement in the desert in Rajasthan which evokes so many comparisons with biblical geography and similar struggles of poor farmers with whom both Jesus and Isaiah related. One of the agencies with whom we worked, AFPRO (Action for Food Production) told us that they (as was Gandhi in his day) are dedicated to the native wisdom of India's rural communities. 'Frugality', said their leader, 'is India's tradition. Modernity sees frugality as poverty.'[28] Tellingly, a key study for the future of the water systems of the desert is entitled *Dying Wisdom*.[29] Desert peoples have their own ways of coping with water scarcity and food shortage, as they did in the times of the biblical Joseph.[30] But the enormity of consumer demand

---

coupled with the systemic destruction of their self-esteem cause these methods to be 'forgotten'. Sophia-Wisdom should stimulate all learning communities to recognise both what they know and where their ignorance lies.

But Jesus talks with and learns from poor men and women, fisherpeople, and vineyard labourers. He uses the way a farmer sows a crop as a metaphor for the word of God. He takes the image of a woman kneading yeast into a loaf as image of the Kingdom of God. He learns from the Syro-Phoenician woman that his calling is beyond the house of Israel.

Second, the Sophia of Jesus is expressed and grounded as a praxis-pedagogy. It cuts through the dualism of theory and applied knowledge. As the Indian theologian George Soares wrote:

> The educational project of Jesus is . . . a public project . . . [It] is not an academic teaching restricted to the members of a tribal school trained in the Law . . . nor is it a secret religious teaching given only to a select group of initiates, which have been admitted to the covenant of grace.[31]

Just as Isaiah had insisted that the Word of God as Wisdom is effective, 'it shall not return to me empty, but it shall accomplish that which I purpose' (Isaiah 55:11), Jesus as enfleshed word/wisdom is known in the way a community achieves the just ordering of its relations, in the way it embodies the kin/dom of right relation. That means not only the engagement with human rights, but the quality of care for justice *within* church structures, and the privileging of minorities *within* our communities.

Third, it is a wisdom which engages both heart and imagination. 'Did not our hearts burn within us?' cried the disciples after the Emmaus experience (Luke 24:32). I think of the words of George Eliot:

> The only effect I ardently long to produce in my writings

is that those who read them should be better able to imagine and feel the pains of those who differ from themselves in everything but the broad fact of being struggling, erring, human creatures.[32]

If imaginations and hearts are deeply touched, humanity touches the wellsprings of compassion. This is the way, rather than through edicts and enforced obligations, to enter into a qualitative listening, from which desires become changed and transformed. Thus Jesus moves and changes people by engaging their imaginations with his stories of the Good Samaritan, the persistent widow and the rich Dives and poor Lazarus.

Fourth, the wisdom of Jesus is not only that of an individual, but is rooted in the wisdom of the whole messianic community. Jesus learnt from his mother, daughter of wisdom, *sedes sapientiae*, as she had learnt from her mother, the St Anne of tradition. From her, and the faithful women who gathered around him as he died, as well as from the apostles, he learnt the expectations of the Messiah and messianic community. As I have said, we are now trying to recover the symbolic imaginary of women as bearers of wisdom, in a culture where models of spirituality are, with a few exceptions, male. Thus the pre-Reformation motif in art and sculpture of the St Anne/Mary/Jesus, in a specific trinitarian iconography (in Dutch known as Anna-te-Drieen, in Brittany popularised through the cult of St Anne mingled with Celtic traditions), begins to restore this tradition (see Illus. 5).

Recovering the role of women as bearers of wisdom is part of the recovery of the whole community's call to be wisdom communities. As Ghanaian theologian Mercy Amba Oduyoye writes, 'Jesus plus the crowd, men and women, make up the image of God's anointed, the Messiah who brings well-being.'[33] The wisdom of prophetic community is both radical and subversive, as we saw in the way Isaiah kept hope alive in the Babylonian captivity. Ultimately the knowing of Jesus, culminating as it did, in Gethsemane, in the realisation that the path of truth and integrity which led him to challenge the systems, would lead to death, is no less subversive today in the struggle to form communities embodying truth and integrity, when lies, secrets and silence are frequently the preferred option.

Finally, as Christian communities permeated with Sophia-Wisdom, it has got to be through the quality of table fellowship that the drama of hope sustained is pursued and embodied. In Chapter 3 I suggested that the eucharistic imagination is ecclesial imagination in contrast with diseased imaginations of torture and death on the one hand, and in happiness imagined as consumerist paradise on the other. The cultural imaginary of flourishing was explored. Now I make the link between the feast on the holy mountain (Isaiah 25) and the invitation to break bread and drink the cup even as 'the silver cord is snapped and the golden bowl is broken . . . and the breath returns to the God who gave it' (Ecclesiastes 12:6, 7).

But it is exactly here that subversive knowing can be blocked. Here the metaphors of hardness of heart, failure to listen, can cause a eucharistic famine, where there is no nourishment, where God waits in vain to be called. Could it be that Christ still knocks at the door of our churches, offering to eat with us and we do not open (Revelation 3:20)? Is the subversive, cutting edge of the Eucharist still domesticated and tamed? The memory of its roots in the context of endangered life, the endangered context of *innocent* life, which for us now also means the planet itself, seems indeed to be lost in a focus on cultic formalism.

In order that the great vision of the transfiguration of creation, present in the texts of the table fellowship of Jesus, and in the narratives of the Last Supper, can embody hope once more and restore the prophetic cutting edge of Eucharist

The Outrageous Pursuit of Hope

so that we also can 'cry freedom' in the marrow of our bones, the Eucharist itself must be experienced as an invitation *to know subversively*. This, surely, was the knowledge which made Peter cry, 'Lord, to whom shall we go? You have the words of eternal life' (John 6:68), when the teaching on Eucharist was too difficult to accept. Knowing Jesus is consuming wisdom, and this wisdom will ever be in conflict with the knowledge of the dominant powers, as it was in Babylon, in Rome and as it is today.

Such knowledge is never comfortable. But Gethsemane was never a comfortable place, and hope is not recovered by cushioning reality. Like the famous little boy in Hans Andersen's story, who cried out that the Emperor had no clothes on,[34] subversive knowing calls for 'telling it how it really is', and wisdom communities are the safe, graced spaces where the narratives of truth can be heard and recognised. Only then can faith communities celebrate Wisdom's feast.

CONCLUSION: CELEBRATING WISDOM'S FEAST

Because faith communities live between memory and fulfilment, and what sustains us is our hope – and this experienced only in glimpses, in tantalising snatches of its embodiment in a short lifespan – this is no reason why its language and aspirations cannot be outrageous. The transgressive Spirit urges that our hope be unquenchable as we plunge deeper into the mystery of life. What, then, is the desire, the yearning, the eros of Sophia-Wisdom communities at this moment of time?

In celebrating Wisdom's feast we can allow ourselves to be shaken at the very foundations (to use Paul Tillich's expression), and speak the truth from the heart. I think human beings long most of all for an end to violence and the grace to live in peace with neighbour. This enables the re-enchantment of the world, the respect and reverence of the ordinary rhythm of life, so that all triviality is banished, so that we live once more in harmony with the seasons' rhythms and each day's tasks are filled with meaning, our work valued. And here in the West, we want it not only for ourselves, but for every village without water, every polluted city, for desert and mountain stripped bare of trees. We want it not only for privileged Euro-Americans, but for all ethnic groups forming part of our pluralist societies across the world, and all indigenous people with threatened identity.

The re-enchantment of the world stimulates celebration, joy in the work of fostering the growth of vulnerable children, and all creatures of earth community, the work of caring and being cared for, the small breakthroughs to justice, the creation of beauty in public and personal spaces. But let the search go deeper. I think ordinary people, as did the ordinary people of the Isaian community, long for the recovery of the relational heart of the world. The world as we see it – broken-hearted, its compassion withered, eros degraded, ritual and worship half-hearted and apathetic – is composed of communities blocked from each other, because blocked from being in mutually just relation with each other. In the Balkans, tragically, neighbour murdered neighbour. However many pictures of mutilated bodies, or of people grieving for lost loved ones in the wake of hurricanes and earthquakes, are shown on the nightly diet of news, the roots of compassion are not touched because the fragile connections between us are ruptured. Healing these broken connections is a complex task: the concrete praxis of cancelling debts and returning land to its rightful owners, namely the agenda of Jubilee, is one way. And there is a real coalescing of a diversity of communities in this struggle to break the chains. Chapter 3 called for a rediscovery of the power of eucharistic ritual both in revelling in the sheer sensuousness of creation, in developing an *ascesis* of care and responsibility for creation and in practising the eucharistic imagination in transfiguring a broken-hearted world.

A third way is for wisdom communities to recover the language of prophetic lament so that the frozen hearts begin to rediscover their passion for justice, their connection with the whole web of life at its deepest level, through a reconversion to the earth. Prophetic communities, as was outlined in Chapter 1, thrive on the interweaving of judgement, vision, memory and also lament. At the moment it is poets, artists and musicians who set our sacramental imaginations on fire, awakening us to what is lost, destroyed, beyond being saved . . . It can be no coincidence that *Requiem* is a best-selling CD in completely non-religious contexts. I think of the way Preissner's *Requiem for my Friend* – with its haunting *Lacrimosa*, has captured the imagination. 'There are tears of things', as the Roman poet Virgil said,[35] and giving voice to grief over what is lost, who is lost, what can never be, is the seed ground for the rebirth of hope. If public spaces can begin to represent the deepest longings and dreams, and people recognise that their hungering for right relation – interpersonally and structurally – is at last given expression, tangibility and embodiment, there might indeed be something positive for the spirit level of the Dome!

But how, finally, shall we dare to maintain and nourish such hope? It is fitting to end with a last image from Isaiah to light a torch for the millennium. In the very last chapter the prophet again returns to the language of giving birth. (And I have been calling the language of birth-giving the language of the Spirit, seeking for the cracks in culture to give birth to new possibilities.) This time it is the birth of the redeemed city, Jerusalem, and we know that the prophet-poet's own hopes focused on the recovery of Jerusalem:

> Shall I open the womb and not deliver?
> Says the Lord.

Shall I, the one who delivers, shut the womb?

(Isaiah 66:9)

Not only is the redeemed city born, but she is a nurturing parent who will nurse her children. The text shifts from Jerusalem nurturing her children to God as a mother nurturing us, her own children:

> As a mother comforts her child,
>> so will I comfort you;
>> you shall be comforted in Jerusalem.
> You shall see, and your heart shall rejoice;
>> your bodies shall flourish like the grass.

(Isaiah 66:13)

The deepest insight of theology is always the simplest. God's is the initiative in grace. Faith in creation *is* faith in redemption. God is giving birth to the redeemed city, redeeming time and space and broken-heartedness. God is promising flourishing to all earth creatures: 'your bodies shall flourish like grass.' Is this is enough to keep us hoping, keep us dreaming, outrageously, for a future for this earth, a cosmic integrity, a future that God offers to all the children of Sophia-Spirit?

A people walking in darkness have seen a great light. There is and can only be one thing that keeps the light burning – *and that is hope* (see Illus. 6).

NOTES

Introduction

1. These were the words of the Foreign Secretary, Edward Grey, on his return from the House of Commons in 1914, where he had just delivered his speech, declaring that the country was at war. See G. M. Trevelyan, *Grey of Fallodon* (London: Longman, Green and Co., 1937), p. 266.
2. George Frederick Watts, 1897. The picture, though not always on display, is frequently in demand for exhibitions.
3. Hesiod, *Works and Days*, ll. 47–105.
4. The Dome is being constructed at Greenwich in an atmosphere of contention over its cost, aesthetic aspects, pollution and traffic considerations, as well as over what should be the content of the 'Spirit Level'. See Chapter 4.
5. John F. A. Sawyer, *The Fifth Gospel: Isaiah in the History of Christianity* (Cambridge: Cambridge University Press, 1996).
6. The idea of a 'female imaginary' means a set of symbols arising from and stimulating the personal, cultural and structural embodiment of women's ways of becoming and being whole. These are in sharp contrast with the necrophilic, patriarchal symbols which have dominated so-called civilised life.

Chapter 1: 'IN MY BEGINNING IS MY END': APOCALYPSE AND THE REBIRTH OF TIME

1. T. S. Eliot, *East Coker* in *Collected Poems 1909–62* (London: Faber & Faber, 1963); see also *Little Gidding* V, 1–3 in the same collection:

   > What we call the beginning is often the end
   > And to make an end is to make a beginning.
   > The end is where we start from.

2. Ruth Gledhill, 'A Place for God amid the Cash Tills', *The Times*, 20 March 1999.
3. Sharon Welch, *A Feminist Ethic of Risk* (Minneapolis, MN: Augsburg Fortress, 1992).

4. John Paul II, *Tertio Millennio Adveniente* (1996), Section 10.
5. Mercy Amba Oduyoye, *African Women-Centred Theology* (Sheffield: Sheffield Academic Press, forthcoming).
6. William Lynch, *Images of Hope* (Notre Dame, IN: University of Notre Dame Press, 1974), p. 32.
7. See Brian Keenan, *An Evil Cradling* (London: Vintage, 1993); John McCarthy and Jill Morrell, *Some Other Rainbow* (London: Corgi Books, 1994).
8. Han Suyin, *The Crippled Tree* (St Albans: Panther Books, 1972); *And the Rain my Drink* (St Albans: Panther Books, 1973); *The Many-Splendoured Thing* (Harmondsworth: Penguin, 1959); *The Morning Deluge: Mao Tse Tung and the Chinese Revolution* (St Albans: Panther Books, 1976).
9. Dzevad Karahasan, *Sarajevo, Exodus of a City*, tr. Slobodan Drakulic (New York: Kodansha International, 1994).
10. Jürgen Moltmann, *Theology of Hope* (1964), tr. John Bowden (London: SCM Press, 1967).
11. Moltmann, *Theology of Hope*, p. 40.
12. See Ian Linden, *Liberation Theology: Coming of Age* (London: CIIR, 1996). It was remarkable that at a recent conference on 'the Future of Liberation Theology' (Birmingham, Newman College, 1999), a conference which attracted over 250 people, the dispute was not over whether liberation theology had a future, but what kind of critique and response it could give in a context of globalisation and unregulated capitalism.
13. Ed de la Torre, unpublished lecture, CIIR Conference, London, Regent's College, 1988.
14. This is explored in Chapter 2.
15. Catherine Keller, *Apocalypse Now and Then: A Feminist Story of the End of the World* (Boston: Beacon, 1996), p. 134.
16. T. S. Eliot, *East Coker* V, 21–3:

> Not the intense moment
> Isolated, with no before or after,
> But a lifetime burning in every moment . . .

17. Emily Dickinson, second stanza of 'Behind Me – dips Eternity – ', *The Complete Poems*, ed. Thomas H. Johnson (London: Faber & Faber, 1975), No. 721, pp. 363–4.
18. Cited in Keller, *Apocalypse Now and Then*, p. 129.
19. Paula Gunn Allen, cited in Keller, *Apocalypse Now and Then*, p. 118.
20. Jürgen Moltmann, *The Coming of God: Christian Eschatology* (1995; ET London: SCM Press, 1996), p. 35.
21. Emily Dickinson, 'Behind Me – dips Eternity – ' (first stanza), *The Complete Poems*, No. 721, pp. 353–4.
22. Catherine Keller, 'Women against Wasting the World' in Irene Diamond and Gloria Feman Orenstein, *Reweaving the World: The Emergence of Ecofeminism* (San Francisco: Sierra Books, 1990), p. 250: 'Waste her! Go ahead, use 'er up! Devastate, consume, expend, squander, ravage, Daddy will give us a new one. The final rapture is almost here!'

---

23. Keller, *Apocalypse Now and Then*, p. 20.
24. Hildegarde of Bingen, *Scivias*, tr. Columba Hart and Jane Bishop (Mahwah, NJ: Paulist Press, 1990), p. 351.
25. See Andrew Bradstock, *Faith in the Revolution* (London: SPCK, 1997).
26. Mark Henderson, 'Botticelli's Millennial Apocalypse – and how!', *The Times*, 21 November 1998.
27. Quoted in Henderson, 'Botticelli's Millennial Apocalypse'.
28. Adrienne Rich, 'The Spirit of Place' in *A Wild Patience Has Taken Me This Far: Poems 1978–1981* (New York: W. W. Norton, 1981), p. 44. Copyright © 1981 by Adrienne Rich. Reprinted by permission of the author and W. W. Norton & Company, Inc.
29. The kind of knowledge that emerges specifically from *ecological* wisdom and the ethics springing from it will be explored in Chapter 3.
30. May Sarton, 'Kali', from *The Mustard Seed* (New York: W. W. Norton, 1971), cited in *Journal of a Solitude* (London: The Women's Press Ltd, 34 Great Sutton Street, London, EC1V 0LQ, 1985), p. 56. Used by permission.
31. T. S. Eliot, *East Coker* III, 23–4, in *Collected Poems 1909–62* (London: Faber & Faber, 1963).
32. Cited in Keller, *Apocalypse Now and Then*, p. 125.
33. Cf. Charles Dickens, *A Tale of Two Cities* (1859), Book I, Ch. 1: 'It was the best of times, it was the worst of times . . .'
34. Matilda Elena Lopez, quoted and translated by Mary de Shazer, *A Poetics of Resistance* (Ann Arbor, MI: University of Michigan Press, 1994), p. 77, cited in Keller, *Apocalypse Now and Then*, p. 124.
35. Wells for India is a small NGO founded by Nicholas Grey, Ramsahai Purohit and myself in 1987, in the context of a terrible drought in the desert of Rajasthan. It is now based in three different areas of this desert and has developed medical, social and educational projects in addition to the original focus on water. The children described here are the children of Project Asha, for whom there is a special educational project.
36. This, the words of Yehuda Amicai, is cited as an Isaianic midrash by Daniel Berrigan, in *Isaiah: Spirit of Courage, Gift of Tears* (Minneapolis, MI: Fortress, 1994), p. 42.
37. Leonardo Boff, *Teologica del Cautivero y de la Liberacion* (Madrid: Ediciones Paulinas, 1978).

Chapter 2: CRYING FREEDOM WHEN THE DREAM HAS DIED: SUBVERSIVE TEXTS AND THE STRUGGLE FOR SURVIVAL

1. Alan Paton, *Cry, the Beloved Country* (Harmondsworth: Penguin, 1948). See also, *Ah, but Your Land is Beautiful* (Harmondsworth: Penguin, 1981).
2. Anne Paton, 'Fly the Beloved Country', *The Sunday Times*, 2 November 1998 (News Review).
3. This is the title of a PhD dissertation by the Dutch theologian Lieve Troch, recently appointed Professor of Feminist Theology in São Paolo,

Brazil. She in turn had taken the title as a variant on Alice Walker's *Possession Is the Secret of Joy* (London: Vintage, 1993).

4. Ivar Lissnar, 'Babylon was Well Lit at Night' in *The Living Past* (London: Jonathan Cape, 1957), p. 41.

5. I am not alone in this. There is now a trend moving away from earlier assumptions. See Walter Brueggemann, *Hopeful Imagination: Prophetic Voices in Exile* (Philadelphia: Fortress, 1986).

6. Gabriele Dietrich, 'The World as the Body of God: Feminist Perspectives on Ecology and Social Justice', *Ecotheology* 5 & 6, pp. 25–50.

7. Walter Brueggemann, *A Social Reading of the Old Testament* (Minneapolis, MI: Fortress, 1994).

8. Chung Hyun Kyung, 'Your Comfort versus My Death' in Mary John Mananzan *et al.* (eds), *Women Resisting Violence: A Spirituality for Life* (Maryknoll, NY: Orbis, 1996), pp. 129–40.

9. Cited in Paula M. Cooey, *Religious Imagination and the Body* (New York and Oxford: OUP, 1994), p. 3.

10. See *I, Rigoberta Menchu* (Barcelona: 1983, London: Verso Editions, 1984), as told to Elizabeth Debray, translated by Ann Wright.

11. Judith Plaskow, *Standing Again at Sinai: Judaism from a Feminist Perspective* (San Francisco: Harper & Row, 1990), pp. 151–69.

12. Plaskow, *Standing Again at Sinai*, p. 151.

13. Kazoh Kitamori, *The Theology of the Pain of God* (London: SCM Press and Richmond, VA: John Knox Press, 1966).

14. Jonathan Andrew, 'AIDS Is a Spiritual Disease', *The Tablet* (28 November 1998), p. 1570.

15. Carter Heyward, 'Passion' in *Our Passion for Justice* (New York: Pilgrim Press, 1984), p. 21.

16. Beverly Wildung Harrison, 'The Power of Anger in the Work of Love' in *Making the Connections: Essays in Feminist Social Ethics*, ed. Carol Robb (Boston: Beacon Press, 1986), p. 15.

17. Aung San Suu Kyi, 'Heavenly Abodes and Human Development', the CAFOD Paul VI Memorial Lecture, 1997. She is actually quoting Sayadav U Pandita, *In This Very Life* (Kandy, 1991), p. 284. It is fitting to cite her here with respect, as, in the course of my delivering the lectures on which this book is based, her husband, Michael Aris, died of cancer without being allowed to see her for the last time. It was Michael Aris who had delivered her lecture in 1997, she being refused permission to travel.

18. Wendy Farley, *Tragic Vision and Divine Compassion: A Contemporary Theodicy* (Louisville, KY: Westminster John Knox Press, 1990).

19. Vandana Shiva, unpublished talk, given at St James's Church, Piccadilly, London, in 1996.

20. See M. Grey, 'The Silence of God in the Face of Evil: A Reflection on the Irish Famine' in *Doctrine and Life* Vol. 66, Part 1, February 1996, Part 2, March 1996.

21. See William Dalrymple, *From the Holy Mountain; A Journey in the Shadow of Byzantium* (London: Flamingo, 1998).

22. Alexander Carmichael (ed.), *Carmina Gadelica* III (Scottish Academic Press, 1976), p. 351.
23. *CIIR News* (October 1998), p. 2.
24. Ian Linden in *CIIR News* (October 1998), p. 4.
25. John Vidal, 'A Dance in the Shadow of Death', *The Guardian* (22 September 1998), p. 2 (G2).

Chapter 3: PROPHETIC IMAGINATION AND THE NOURISHING OF EARTH COMMUNITIES

1. The classic text is Mary Warnock, *Imagination* (London: Faber, 1976). See also David Tracy, *The Analogical Imagination* (New York: Crossroad, 1981); Philip Keane, *Christian Ethics and Imagination* (New York: Paulist Press, 1984). For feminist theology, see Paula Cooey, *Religious Imagination and the Body: A Feminist Analysis* (New York and Oxford: OUP, 1994); Sharon Welch, *A Feminist Ethic of Risk* (Minneapolis, MN: Augsburg Fortress, 1990).
2. Walter Brueggemann, *The Prophetic Imagination* (Philadelphia: Fortress, 1978).
3. Maria Harris, *Proclaim Jubilee: A Spirituality for the 21st Century* (Louisville, KY: Westminster John Knox Press, 1996), p. 4. I used this quotation as inspiration for a keynote paper for the (Roman Catholic) Justice and Peace National Conference, Swanwick (Derbyshire), 1998.
4. Harris, *Proclaim Jubilee*, p. 15.
5. See M. Grey, *Beyond the Dark Night: A Way Forward for the Church?* (London: Cassell, 1997), Ch. 1.
6. David S. Toolan, 'Praying in a Post-Einsteinian Universe', *Crosscurrents* (Winter 1996/7), pp. 437–77, quotation on p. 435.
7. Toolan is here citing Abraham Heschel, *The Sabbath: Its Meaning for Modern Man* (New York: Farrar, Straus & Giroux, 1951), p. 8 and *passim*.
8. Martha Nussbaum, *Poetic Justice: The Literary Imagination and Public Life* (Boston: Beacon, 1995).
9. See M. Grey, *Beyond the Dark Night*, ch. 8, 'Dreaming'.
10. Elisabeth Schüssler Fiorenza, *Bread not Stone: The Challenge of Feminist Biblical Interpretation* (Edinburgh: T. & T. Clark, 1984), p. xiii: 'Reclaiming the Bible as a feminist heritage and resource is only possible because it has not functioned only to legitimate the oppression of all women: freeborn, slave, black and white . . . It has also provided authorisation and legitimisation for women who have rejected slavery, racism, anti-semitism, colonial exploitation and misogynism as unbiblical and against God's will. The Bible has inspired countless women to speak out and to struggle against injustice, exploitation and stereotyping.'
11. Interestingly, Lilith appears in Kabbalistic folklore, but also in modern Jewish literature. See Amoz Oz, *Where the Jackals Howl* (New York: Harcourt, Brace, Jovanovich, 1981). See my discussion of Lilith in 'All

---

about Eve' in Martyn Percy (ed.), *Intimate Affairs* (London: Darton, Longman & Todd, 1997), pp. 86–94.

12. Joan Chittister, *Woman Strength: Modern Church* (London: Sheed & Ward, 1990), pp. 69–70.

13. Walter Brueggemann, *The Bible and the Postmodern Imagination* (London: SCM Press, 1993), ch. 2.

14. This is not to suggest that this is the only source for prophetic imagination. But it must count as a privileged source of nourishment for Jewish and Christian communities.

15. Brian Swimme, *The Heart of the Universe* (video).

16. I have discussed this in M. Grey, *Prophecy and Mysticism: the Heart of the Postmodern Church* (Edinburgh: T. & T. Clark, 1997), pp. 70–3.

17. Brueggemann, *The Bible*, ch. 2.

18. Gila Gevirtz, cover of *Cross Currents*, Winter 1997–1998.

19. See *Letter to the Churches* (Geneva: WCC, 1992), p. 10.

20. For a historical account of the Church's involvement in ecological issues, see Donald Bruce and David Pickering, 'Ecology and Ecumenism in Europe: A Way Forward', *Ecotheology* 5 & 6 (January 1999), pp. 9–21.

21. Gwyn Prins, 'The Challenge of Ecology' in Alan Race and Roger Williamson (eds), *True to This Earth* (Oxford: Oneworld Publications, 1995), pp. 14–27.

22. Prins, 'Challenge of Ecology', p. 19.

23. Prins, 'Challenge of Ecology', p. 27.

24. See, for example, Grace Jantzen, *Becoming Divine: Towards a Feminist Philosophy of Religion* (Manchester: Manchester University Press, 1998); Chris J. Cuomo, *Feminism and Ecological Communities* (London: Routledge, 1998). See the discussion of Martha Nussbaum and Amartya Sen on capabilities/functioning and in relation to flourishing (*Women, Culture and Development*, ed. M. Nussbaum and J. Glover, OUP, 1995). Here the women consulted by OXFAM as to choice of a particular project over and above others focused on the fact that the women had chosen the rose-growing project – even though the economic gain was the same – because the experience of working with roses was pleasurable and the scent of the roses stayed with them when they had finished.

25. Jill Paton Walsh, *A Knowledge of Angels* (London: Black Swan, 1998).

26. This is to build on the fact that the Isaian text has been continually reworked for different contexts right through the Christian tradition.

27. For Wells for India see Chapter 1, note 35. From concentrating on ensuring clean drinking water for desert communities in Rajasthan, we moved into integrated social work – education, medical, women's projects and long-term water harvesting.

28. Alvin Pitcher, *Listen to the Crying of the Earth: Cultivating Creation Communities* (Cleveland, OH: Pilgrim Press, 1993).

29. This refers to the Chipko movement: in 1730 Amrita Devi, who lived in a Bishnoi village in Rajasthan, attempted to prevent the Maharaja of Jodhpur's soldiers from chopping down trees by throwing her arms around them (Chipko means tree-hugging). She and 363 Bishnoi people were

hacked to pieces. She is known as the leader of the Chipko movement, now a powerful movement in India and other parts of the world, acting on the same inspiration. For example, the Chipko Andolan movement 'is a movement in which both village women and men participate as leaders. It now spans the whole Himalayan region. On their marches . . . Chipko activists came into contact with the societies of remote hill areas. Their message of anguish about the ecological situation of the region began to spread as more and more people and villages became involved.' Irene Dankelman and Joan Davidson, *Women and Environment in the Third World: Alliance for the Future* (London: Earthscan Publications, 1988), p. 49.

30. St Maximus the Confessor, *Mystagogy* 5, cited in Vincent Rossi, 'Liturgising the World', *Ecotheology* 3 (July 1997), p. 81.

31. David Toolan, 'Praying in a post-Einsteinian Universe', *Crosscurrents* Vol. 64, No. 4 (Winter 1996–7), pp. 468–9.

32. William Cavanaugh, *Torture and Eucharist* (Oxford: Blackwell, 1998).

33. Richard Woods, 'The Seven Bowls of Wrath: An Ecological Parable', *Ecotheology* 7 (1999), pp. 8–21.

34. There are of course some encouraging signs that communities with their bishops are making themselves accountable for the ravaging of land and plight of indigenous people. I think of the lifelong work of the late Bishop Helder Camara in Brazil (see Bishops Conference of Brazil, *Liberate the Land* (London: CIIR, 1986), and the lifelong work of Sean McDonagh in the Philippines (see Sean McDonagh, *Passion for the Earth* (London: Geoffrey Chapman, 1994)).

Chapter 4: THE RE-EMERGENCE OF THE SPIRIT: A NEW LANGUAGE OF THE SACRED IN A POSTMODERN WORLD

1. The reference is, of course to Samuel Taylor Coleridge's poem, 'Kubla Khan' (1816), lines 1–5:

> In Xanadu did Kubla Khan
> A stately pleasure-dome decree:
> Where Alph, the sacred river, ran
> Through caverns measureless to man
> Down to a sunless sea.

2. Teletubbies, with their bland, featureless faces, seem to be a poignant symbol for the collapsed identity of our age.

3. This was the phrase of Fr Philip Da Silva (from New Orleans), quoting the theologian Gerry Boodoo (also a participant and speaker).

4. See M. Grey, ' "Expelled again from Eden": Facing Difference through Connection', *Feminist Theology* No. 21 (May 1999), pp. 8–21.

5. Michel Foucault, *Power/Knowledge: Selected Interviews and Other Writings, 1972–1977*, tr. C. Gordon, L. Marshall and J. Mepham (New York and London: Pantheon, 1990), p. 81.

6. Gerald Priestland, 'The Guest who Came to Dinner' in *Priestland's Progress* (London: BBC Publications, 1981).

7. I do not dwell here on phenomena such as the 'Toronto Blessing' – my main aim is to understand the theology of the Spirit in relation to the spirit of the age.

8. Harvey Cox, *Fire from Heaven* (London: Cassell, 1996).

9. Cox, *Fire from Heaven*, p. 314.

10. Cox, *Fire from Heaven*, p. 315.

11. John Taylor, *The Go-Between God* (London: Collins, 1972).

12. Jemima Wilkinson, Document 14 in Rosemary Ruether and Catherine M. Prelinger, 'Women in Sectarian and Utopian Groups' in *The Colonial and Revolutionary Periods: A Documentary History*, Vol. 2 of *Women and Religion in America*, ed. R. R. Ruether and R. S. Keller (San Francisco: Harper & Row, 1983), p. 512. Cited in Keller, *Apocalypse Now and Then*, p. 234.

13. 'Like a bird hanging in the air over its young in the nest, Deut. 32:11': JB note c on Genesis 1:1.

14. See M. Grey, *The Wisdom of Fools?* (London: SPCK, 1993).

15. Think of what the theology of androgynous being has meant for the theology of marriage – two half beings wandering around until they cleave to each other and produce one whole being! This hardly offers the fullness of human identity for single people.

16. See Mark Wallace, *Fragments of the Spirit: Nature, Violence and the Renewal of Creation* (New York: Continuum, 1996), ch. 5 'The Wild Bird Who Heals', pp. 133–70.

17. I leave here the mythological suggestion that the *tohu bohu*/the *tehom* of chaos is linked etymologically with Tiamat, the slaughtered mother goddess, at the core of the *Enuma Elish*, the Babylonian epic of creation, and therefore that there is a cosmic matricide at the heart of the creation story.

18. Elizabeth Johnson, 'Remembering Creator Spirit' in Joann Wolski Conn (ed.), *Women's Spirituality: Resources for Christian Development* (New York: Paulist, 1986, revised edn 1996), p. 372 (1996 edn). She is citing Hildegarde, *Scivias*, tr. Columba Hart and Jane Bishop (New York: Paulist Press, 1990), p. 190 and *passim*.

19. Taylor, *Go-Between God*, p. 11.

20. Edwin Muir, *Collected Poems* (London: Faber & Faber, 1960), pp. 223–4; cited in Taylor, *Go-Between God*, p. 11.

21. Carter Heyward, *The Redemption of God: A Theology of Mutual Relation* (Washington: University of America Press, 1980), p. 172.

22. Sallie McFague, *The Body of God* (London: SCM Press, 1993).

23. Davies, cited by Walter Schwarz, *The Guardian*, 6 April 1987.

24. Martin Heidegger, 'The Question concerning Technology' in *Basic Writings*, ed. D. Krell (New York: Harper & Row, 1977).

25. For example at the scene of the Hillsborough football disaster, and after the death of Diana, Princess of Wales.

26. In India the follower of Gandhi, the late Vinoba Bhave, famous for the

day. See Vinoba Bhave, *Moved by Love*, tr. M. Sykes (Dartington: Resurgence, 1994).

27. See Wallace, *Fragments of the Spirit*, p. 146.

28. Wallace, *Fragments of the Spirit*, p. 145.

29. Wallace, *Fragments of the Spirit*, p. 228.

30. Mark 3:28–30; Luke 12:10; Hebrews 6:4; 10:24.

31. John Milton, *Paradise Lost* (1667), Bk 4, 108–10, *John Milton: A Critical Edition of the Major Works*, ed. S. Orgel and J. Goldberg (Oxford: OUP, 1991):

> So farewell hope, and with hope, farewell fear,
> Farewell remorse! All good to me is lost;
> Evil, be thou my good.

32. The discussion is influenced by Scripture texts like that of the eunuch of Acts 8 having the text interpreted for him by Philip, and then immediately proceeding to baptism.

33. I refer to the discussion in William Bellinger Jr and William R. Farmer (eds), *Jesus and the Suffering Servant* (Harrisburg: Trinity Press International, 1998).

34. T. S. Eliot, *Ash Wednesday*, l. 174, *Collected Poems* (London: Faber and Faber, 1974), p. 103.

35. From *Confessing Our Faith Around the World IV, South America* (WCC, 1985), quoted in Janet Morley (ed.), *Bread of Tomorrow* (SPCK and Christian Aid, 1993), p. 133–4.

36. Chung Hyun Kyung, 'Welcome the Spirit: Hear her Cries: The Holy Spirit, Creation and the Culture of Life', *Christianity and Crisis* 51 (15 July), pp. 220–3.

Chapter 5: 'WISDOM'S FEAST': THE CELEBRATION OF COSMIC INTEGRITY

1. Denise Levertov, 'Beginners', quoted in Keller, *Apocalypse Now and Then*, p. 275. ('Beginners' by Denise Levertov, from *Candles in Babylon*. Copyright © 1982 by Denise Levertov. Reprinted by permission of New Directions Publishing Corp/Gerald Pollinger, Ltd.)

2. Elsa Tamez, cited in Anselm Kyongsuk Min's review of *Liberation Theologies, Postmodernity and the Americas*, ed. David Batstone, Eduardo Mendieta, Lois Ann Lorentzen and Dwight N. Hopkins (Routledge, 1997), in *Journal of the American Academy of Religion* Vol. 66, No. 4 (Winter 98), pp. 922–3.

3. Lucy Tatman, 'Wisdom' in L. Isherwood and D. McEwan (eds), *An A to Z of Feminist Theology* (Sheffield: Sheffield Academic Press, 1996), p. 238.

4. For a fuller development of this, see M. Grey, 'The Return of Sophia', *New Blackfriars* (October 1999).

5. For a fuller account, see Susan Cole, Marion Ronan and Hal Taussig,

Wisdom's Feast: Sophia in Study and Celebration (Kansas City: Sheed & Ward, 1996).

6. See Carol Christ, *Diving Deep and Surfacing* (Boston: Beacon Press, 1980); *The Laughter of Aphrodite: Reflections on a Journey to the Goddess* (San Francisco: Harper & Row, 1987).

7. The most negative of all has been the reaction to the Re-imagining Conference in the United States in Minneapolis, 1993. See the discussion in Ninna Edgardh Beckman, 'Sophia: Symbol of Christian and Feminist Wisdom', *Feminist Theology* No. 16 (September 1997), pp. 32–54.

8. See M. Grey, 'Zür Leitung Ermächtigt: Sophias Tochter bahnen den Weg!' in Gertraud Ladner and Michaela Moser (eds), *Frauen Bewegen Europa* (Thaur, Austria: Druck und Verlagshaus Thaur, 1997), pp. 62–77.

9. See Celia Deane-Drummond, 'Sophia: The Feminine Face of God as a Metaphor for Ecotheology', *Feminist Theology* No. 16 (September 1997), pp. 11–31.

10. Andrew Louth, 'Wisdom and the Russians' in Stephen Barton (ed.), *Where Shall Wisdom Be Found?* (Edinburgh: T. & T. Clark, 1998), p. 173.

11. Deane-Drummond, 'Sophia', p. 16.

12. Sergei Bulgakov, *The Wisdom of God: A Brief Summary of Sophiology* (New York: The Paisley Press; London: Williams and Norgate, 1937).

13. Bulgakov, *Wisdom of God*, p. 39. Cited in Louth, 'Wisdom and the Russians', pp. 176–7.

14. M. Grey, *The Wisdom of Fools?* (London: SPCK, 1993).

15. Celia Deane-Drummond, *Theology and Biotechnology: Implications for a New Science* (London: Geoffrey Chapman, 1997).

16. See Anne Carr, *A Search for Wisdom and Spirit: Thomas Merton's Theology of the Self* (Notre Dame, IN: University of Notre Dame Press, 1988), p. 71.

17. Elisabeth Schüssler Fiorenza, *Jesus, Miriam's Child, Sophia's Prophet* (London: SCM Press, 1995). But of course the idea was first introduced in her earlier work, *In Memory of Her* (London: SCM Press, 1980).

18. Elizabeth Johnson, *She Who Is* (New York: Crossroad, 1994).

19. T. S. Eliot, *East Coker* III, 23–4 in *Collected Poems 1909–62* (London: Faber & Faber, 1963).

20. Susan Griffin, 'This Earth is My Sister' in Judith Plaskow and Carol Christ (eds), *Weaving the Visions* (New York: Harper & Row, 1989), p. 107.

21. Susan Griffin, *Made from this Earth: Selections from her Writings* (London: The Women's Press, 1982), p. 88.

22. Joanna Macy, citing Symeon the New Theologian, in *Interchange: Journal of Creation Spirituality* (Winter 1998), p. 4.

23. *Kairos Europa* document, Sarum College Press 1998, p. 41 (my italics).

24. For example, in the Jesse Tree of Hildegarde of Bingen. See Isaiah 11:1–3.

25. This is well argued in Asphodel Long, *In a Chariot Drawn by Lions* (London: The Women's Press, 1992).

26. Sophia-Wisdom, it is true – and this was remarked in the discussion following the lecture on which this was based – is drawn from secular

contexts. In addition some of the texts in which she appears – although this is not true of Isaiah – are not women-friendly. I think it needs to be said that we draw on Sophia texts in a different way from some of the original contexts. But if linking them with liberation and justice contexts is a development of the original, it is certainly not hostile or a distortion of the more ancient root.

27. Paolo Freire, *Pedagogy of Hope* (New York: Continuum, 1996), pp. 46–7.

28. The source is a speech made by Mr Devangan, AFPRO's leader, to Wells for India, on a visit to Udaipur, January 1999.

29. *Dying Wisdom: The Rise and Fall and Potential of India's Traditional Water-Harvesting Systems*, ed. Anil Agarwal and Sunita Naraina (New Delhi: Centre for Science and the Environment, 1996).

30. 'And since the famine had spread over all the land, Joseph opened all the storehouses, and sold to the Egyptians, for the famine was severe in the land of Egypt . . .' (Genesis 41:56).

31. George Soares-Prabhu, 'Jesus the Teacher: The Liberative Pedagogy of Jesus of Nazareth' in *Jeeva dhara* Vol. 12, No. 69, p. 243.

32. Cited by Wendy Farley, in the acknowledgement page of *Eros for the Other: Retaining Truth in a Pluralist Society* (Philadelphia, PA: University of Pennsylvania State Press, 1996).

33. Mercy Amba Oduyoye, *Women-Centred Theology of African Women* (Sheffield: Sheffield Academic Press, forthcoming).

34. Hans Christian Andersen, 'The Emperor's New Clothes' in *Andersen's Fairy Tales* (London: Dent and Sons Ltd, 1899), p. 294: ' "But he has got nothing on," said a little child.'

35. *Sunt lacrimae rerum*, Virgil, *Aeneid*, Bk 1.462.

FURTHER READING

Isaiah and Material on Hebrew Prophecy

Bellinger, William Jr and Farmer, William R. (eds), *Jesus and the Suffering Servant* (Harrisburg: Trinity Press International, 1998).

Berrigan, Daniel, *Isaiah, Spirit of Courage, Gift of Tears* (Minneapolis, MN: Fortress Press, 1996).

Brueggemann, Walter, *The Prophetic Imagination* (Minneapolis: Fortress Press, 1979).

—— *A Social Reading of the Old Testament* (Minneapolis, MN: Fortress, 1994).

—— *Hopeful Imagination: Prophetic Voices in Exile* (Philadelphia; Fortress Press, 1986).

—— *Isaiah 1—39* (Louisville, KY: Westminster John Knox Press, 1998).

—— *Isaiah 40—66* (Louisville, KY: Westminster John Knox Press, 1998).

Kaiser, Otto, *Isaiah*, tr. John Bowden (London: SCM Press, 1983).

Sawyer, John, *The Fifth Gospel: Isaiah in the History of Christianity* (Cambridge: Cambridge University Press, 1996).

Westermann, Klaus, *Isaiah 40—66* (London: SCM Press, 1969).

General

Barton, Stephen (ed.), *Where Shall Wisdom be Found?* (Edinburgh: T. & T. Clark, 1998).

Bauckham, Richard and Hart, Trevor, *Hope against Hope: Christian Eschatology in Contemporary Context* (London: Darton, Longman & Todd, 1999).

Bhave, Vinoba, *Moved by Love* (Dartington: Resurgence, 1994).

Beckman, Ninna Edgardh, 'Sophia: Symbol of Christian and Feminist Wisdom?', *Feminist Theology* No. 16 (September 1997), pp. 32–54.

Bradstock, Andrew, *Faith in the Revolution* (London: SPCK, 1997).

Cavanaugh, William, *Torture and the Eucharist* (Oxford: Blackwell, 1998).

Chittister, Joan, *Woman Strength: Modern Church* (London: Sheed & Ward, 1990).

Christ, Carol, *Diving Deep and Surfacing* (Boston, MA: Beacon Press, 1980).

—— *The Laughter of Aphrodite: Reflections on a Journey to the Goddess* (San Francisco, CA: Harper & Row, 1987).

Chung, Hyun Kyung, 'Welcome the Spirit: Hear her Cries', *Christianity and Crisis* 51 (15 July), pp. 220–3.

Cole, Susan, Ronan, Marion and Taussig, Hal, *Wisdom's Feast: Sophia in Study and Celebration* (Kansas City, KS: Sheed & Ward, 1996).

Cooey, Paula M., *Religious Imagination and the Body* (New York and Oxford: OUP, 1994).

Cox, Harvey, *Fire from Heaven* (London: Cassell, 1996).

Cuomo, Chris J., *Feminism and Ecological Communities* (London: Routledge, 1998).

Deane-Drummond, Celia, *Theology and Biotechnology: Implications for a New Science* (London: Geoffrey Chapman, 1997).

Echlin, Edward, *Earth Spirituality: Jesus at the Centre* (New Alresford: Arthur James, 1999).

Farley, Wendy, *Tragic Vision and Divine Compassion: A Contemporary Theodicy* (Louisville, KY: Westminster John Knox Press, 1990).

Fiorenza, Elisabeth Schüssler, *Bread not Stone: The Challenge of Feminist Biblical Interpretation* (Edinburgh: T. & T. Clark, 1984).

—— *Jesus, Miriam's Child, Sophia's Prophet* (London: SCM Press, 1996).

Freire, Paolo, *Pedagogy of Hope* (New York: Continuum, 1996).

Grey, Mary, *Redeeming the Dream* (London: SPCK, 1989).

—— *The Wisdom of Fools?* (London: SPCK, 1993).

—— *Beyond the Dark Night: A Way Forward for the Church?* (London: Cassell, 1997).

—— *Prophecy and Mysticism: The Heart of the Postmodern Church* (Edinburgh: T. & T. Clark, 1997).

Griffin, Susan, *Made from this Earth: Selections from her Writings* (London: The Women's Press, 1982).

Harris, Maria, *Proclaim Jubilee: A Spirituality for the 21st Century* (Louisville, KY: Westminster John Knox Press, 1996).

Heyward, Carter, *Our Passion for Justice* (New York: Pilgrim Press, 1984

—— *The Redemption of God: A Theology of Mutual Relation* (Washington, DC: University of America Press, 1980).

Hildegarde of Bingen, *Scivias*, tr. Columba Hart and Jane Bishop (Mahwah, NJ: Paulist Press, 1990).

Jantzen, Grace, *Becoming Divine: Towards a Feminist Philosophy of Religion* (Manchester: MUP, 1998).

Johnson, Elizabeth, *She Who Is* (New York: Crossroad, 1994).

Keane, Philip, *Christian Ethics and Imagination* (New York: Paulist Press, 1984).

Keller, Catherine, *Separation, Sexism and the Self* (Boston, MA: Beacon Press, 1986).

—— *Apocalypse Now and Then: A Feminist Story of the End of the World* (Boston, MA: Beacon Press, 1996).

Kitamori, Kazoh, *The Theology of the Pain of God* (London: SCM Press and Richmond, VA: John Knox Press, 1966).

Lane, Dermot, *Keeping Hope Alive: Stirrings in Christian Theology* (Dublin: Gill & Macmillan, 1996).

Linden, Ian, *Liberation Theology – Coming of Age?* (London: CIIR, 1997).

Further Reading

Lissnar, Ivar, *The Living Past* (London: Jonathan Cape, 1957).

Long, Asphodel, *In a Chariot Drawn by Lions* (London: The Women's Press, 1992).

Lynch, William, *Images of Hope* (Notre Dame, IN: University of Notre Dame Press, 1974).

McFague, Sallie, *The Body of God* (London: SCM Press, 1993).

Mananzan, Mary John et al., *Women Resisting Violence: A Spirituality for Life* (Maryknoll, NY: Orbis, 1996).

McKelvey, R. J., *The Millennium and the Book of Revelation* (Cambridge: Lutterworth Press, 1999).

Moltmann, Jürgen, *Theology of Hope* (London: SCM Press, 1967).

—— *The Coming of God: Christian Eschatology* (London: SCM Press, 1996).

—— *Is There Life after Death?* The Père Marquette Lecture 1998 (Milwaukee, WI: Marquette University Press, 1998).

Nussbaum, Martha, *Poetic Justice: The Literary Imagination and Public Life* (Boston, MA: Beacon Press, 1995).

Oduyoye, Mercy Amba, *Women-Centred Theology of African Women* (Sheffield: Sheffield Academic Press, forthcoming).

Pitcher, Alvin, *Listen to the Crying of the Earth: Cultivating Creation Communities* (Cleveland, OH: Pilgrim Press, 1993).

Plaskow, Judith, *Standing Again at Sinai: Judaism from a Feminist Perspective* (San Francisco: Harper & Row, 1990).

Plaskow, Judith and Christ, Carol (eds), *Weaving the Visions* (New York: Harper & Row, 1989).

Taylor, John, *The Go-Between God* (London: Collins, 1972).

Toole, David, *Waiting for Godot in Sarajevo: Theological Reflections on Nihilism, Tragedy and Apocalypse* (Boulder, CO: Westview Press, 1998).

Toolan, David. 'Praying in a Post-Einsteinian Universe', *Crosscurrents* Vol. 46, No. 4 (Winter 1996–7), pp. 468–9.

Wallace, Mark, *Fragments of the Spirit: Nature, Violence and the Renewal of Creation* (New York: Continuum, 1996).

Warnock, Mary, *Imagination* (London: Faber & Faber, 1976).

Welch, Sharon, *A Feminist Ethic of Risk* (Philadelphia: Fortress Press, 1978).

Wilshire, Bruce, *Wild Hunger: The Primal Roots of Modern Addiction* (Oxford, MD: Rowman & Littlefield, 1998).

Woods, Richard, 'The Seven Bowls of Wrath: An Ecological Parable', *Ecotheology* 7 (1999), pp. 8–21.

Poetry

Coleridge, Samuel Taylor, 'Kubla Khan' in *The Oxford Book of English Verse*, ed. Arthur Quiller-Couch (Oxford: Clarendon Press, 1925).

Dickinson, Emily, *The Complete Poems*, ed. Thomas H. Johnson (London: Faber & Faber, 1975).

Eliot, T. S. *Collected Poems 1909–62* (London: Faber & Faber, 1963).

Levertov, Denise, 'Beginnings', from *Candles in Babylon* (New York: New Directions Publishing Corp, 1982), cited by Catherine Keller, *Apocalypse Now and Then* (1996).

Milton, John, *Paradise Lost* in *John Milton: A Critical Edition of the Major Works*, ed. S. Orgel and J. Goldberg (Oxford: OUP, 1991).

Morley, Janet (ed.), *Bread of Tomorrow* (London: SPCK and Christian Aid, 1993).

Muir, Edwin, *Collected Poems* (London: Faber & Faber, 1960).

Rich, Adrienne, *A Wild Patience Has Taken Me This Far* (New York: W. W. Norton, 1981).

Sarton, May, *A Grain of Mustard Seed* (New York: W. W. Norton, 1971).

INDEX

Grey, Mary 102 n. 20, 103 n. 5, 104 n. 16, 105
n. 4, 106 n. 14, 107 n. 4
Griffin, Susan 87–8, 108 nn. 20 and 21

Handel's *Messiah* 74
Harris, Maria 40, 103 nn. 3 and 4
Harrison, Beverly Wildung 33, 102 n. 16
Heidegger, Martin 70, 106 n. 24
Henderson, Mark 101 nn. 26 and 27
Hesiod 99 n. 3 (Intro.)
Heyward, Carter 33, 102 n. 15, 106 n. 21
Highland Clearances 35–6
Hildegarde of Bingen 11, 65, 108 n. 24; as
summed up by Elizabeth Johnson 68,106
n. 18

Isaiah xi, 6; and Babylonian exile 22–32; and
compassionate mothering of God 29–31,
97–8; and ecological wisdom 14–16, 51–4,
71; and historicising of hope 12–13; and
prophetic imagination 41, 45–6, 49–57;
and prophetic wisdom of Jesus 86–95; and
resurrection for the earth 49–51; and Sophia
Wisdom 86–95; and the Spirit 71, 73; and
Suffering Servant 74–8

Jantzen, Grace and flourishing 48–9, 104 n. 24
Jesse Tree 90, 108 n. 24
Jesus, the wisdom of 86–95
Joachim of Fiore 11
John Paul II 2, 100 n. 4
Johnson, Elizabeth 85, 106 n. 18, 108 n. 18
Jubilee 16, 77, 90, 96

Kairos Europa 89, 108 n. 23
Karahasan, Dzevad 100 n. 9
Keane, Philip 103 n. 1
Keenan, Brian 3, 100 n. 7
Keller, Catherine 7, 8, 10, 12, 16, 100 nn. 15,
18, 19 and 22, 101 nn. 23, 32 and 34
Kitamori, Kazoh 29, 102 n. 13

Letter to the Churches 104 n. 19
Levertov, Denise 79–80, 107 n. 1
Lilith, demonisation of, in Isaiah 43 103–4
n. 11
Linden, Ian and Memory Project 36–7, 103
n. 24
Lissnar, Ivar 102 n. 4
Long, Asphodel 108 n. 25
Lopez, Matilda Elena 16, 101 n. 34
Louth, Andrew 108 n. 10
Luria, Isaac 40
Lynch, William 2, 100 n. 6

Macy, Joanna 88, 108 n. 22
Maier, Charles 8
Mananzan, Mary John 102 n. 8
Mary, mother of Jesus as Seat of Wisdom 83,
90; in Trinitarian iconography 93
Maximus the Confessor, St 55–6, 105 n. 30

McCarthy, John 3, 100 n. 7
McDonagh, Sean 105 n. 34
McFague, Sallie 69–70, 106 n. 22
Memory Project 36–7
Menchu, Rigoberta 27, 102 n. 10
Merton, Thomas 85, 108 n. 16
Milton, John 107 n. 31
Min, Anselm Kyongsuk 107 n. 2
Moltmann, Jürgen 5, 12, 69, 100 nn. 10, 11
and 20
Morley, Janet 107 n. 35
Muir, Edwin 68–9, 106 n. 20
Murdoch, Iris 15

Nussbaum, Martha 103 n. 8, and Amartya Sen
104 n. 24

Oduyoye, Mercy Amba 2, 93, 100 n. 5, 109
n. 33
OXFAM and rose-growing project 104 n. 24
Oz, Amoz 103 n. 11

Pandora, myth of x
Paradise Lost 73, 107 n. 31
Partnoy, Alicia 26
Paton, Alan 19, 101 n. 1
Paton, Anne 19, 101 n. 2
Pickering, David 104 n. 20
Pitcher, Alvin 104 n. 28
Plaskow, Judith and otherness of God 28, 102
nn. 11 and 12
Plazotta, Carol 12
Preissner's *Requiem for my Friend* 97
Priestland, Gerald 62, 105 n. 6
Prins, Gwyn and approaches to the
environment 46–8, 104 nn. 21–3
Prophetic lament 37, 97

Race, Alan 104 n. 21
Re-imagining Conference (1993) 108 n. 7
Rich, Adrienne 14, 101 n. 28
Ronan, Marian 107 n. 5

Sarton, May 15, 101 n. 30
Savonarola, Girolamo 12
Sawyer, John 99 n. 5
Sen, Amartya 104 n. 24
Shiva, Vandana 34, 102 n. 19
Soares Prabhu, Georges 92, 109 n. 31
Sölle, Dorothee 62
Soloviev, Vladimir 84
Sontag, Susan 3–4
Sophia/Wisdom/Hokmah xii, 24, 79, 81–5;
and Merton's prose-poem Hagia Sophia 85;
origins of 108–9 n. 26; as *phronesis* 88–91;
and *The Wisdom of Fools?* 85, 108 n. 14;
and Wisdom's Feast 95–8
Spirituality of attending to time 14–18; of
prophetic imagination 54; of resistance
32–9; and sacramental imagination 54–7
Suyin, Han 3, 100 n. 8

Index   115

Swimme, Brian 104 n. 15

Tamez, Elsa 80, 107 n. 2
Tatman, Lucy 81, 107 n. 3
Taussig, Hal 107 n. 5
Taylor, John use of Annunciation as
  inspirational motif 68, 106 n. 19; and
  movements of the Spirit 64, 106 n. 11
Teletubbies 59, 105 n. 2
Thürmer-Rohr, Christina 15
tikkun olam 40–1
Tillich, Paul 95
Toolan, David and imagination 41, 103 n. 6;
  and liturgy 56, 105 n. 31
Torre, Ed de la 5, 100 n. 13
Tracy, David 103 n. 1

Troch, Lieve 101–2 n. 3

Virgil's *Aeneid* 97, 109 n. 35

Walker, Alice 102 n. 3
Wallace, Mark 72, 106 n. 16, 107 nn. 27–9
Walsh, Jill Paton 49, 104 n. 25
Warnock, Mary 103 n. 1
Watts, George Frederick ix, 99 n. 2 (Intro.)
Weil, Simone 15
Welch, Sharon 2, 99 n. 3 (Ch. 1); 103 n. 1
Wells for India 17, 50–1, 91–2, 101 n. 35, 104
  n. 27, 109 n. 35
Wilkinson, Jemima 65–6, 106 n. 12
Williamson, Roger 104 n. 21
Woods, Richard 56, 105 n. 33